Stories from Herodotus

adapted and translated by

BRIAN WILSON
and
DAVID MILLER

D1339369

OXFORD UNIVERSITY PRESS

Oxford University Press, Walton Street, Oxford OX2 6DP
OXFORD LONDON GLASGOW
NEW YORK TORONTO MELBOURNE WELLINGTON
KUALA LUMPUR SINGAPORE HONG KONG TOKYO
DELHI BOMBAY CALCUTTA MADRAS KARACHI
NAIROBI DAR ES SALAAM CAPE TOWN

© Oxford University Press 1973

First published 1973
Reprinted 1979

Filmset in 9/12 pt Ionic by
BAS Printers Limited, Over Wallop, Hampshire
and printed in Hong Kong by
Brighter Printing Press Ltd.

Contents

List of Maps

Acknowledgements

We should like to thank the following for permission to reproduce illustrations; Archaeological Museum, Delphi, 33; British Museum, 38, 82; Cliché des Musées Nationaux, (Louvre), 1, 37, 86; Roman Ghirshman, 26, 38, 55, 74; Michael Holford, 56 (top), 67, 69, 71, 104; Kunsthistorisches Museum, Vienna, 93; Mansell, cover, 43, 46, 50, 56, 60, 62, 94, 100; Metropolitan Museum of Art, Harris Brisbane Dick Fund, 1954, 29, Rogers Fund, 1906, 118; Pavlos Myloff, Athens, 127; National Archaeological Museum, Athens, 91; Oriental Institute, University of Chicago, 44, 81; Paul Popper Ltd, 99; Roger-Viollet, 18, 25, 106.

Apologies are offered for any inadvertent breach of copyright in the use of material where it has not proved possible to trace the original copyright-owners.

Introduction

'The purpose of this book is to prevent humanity, as time goes on, from forgetting its own past; to give proper fame to amazing achievements, on the non-Greek side as well as the Greek; and, in particular, to explain why there was a war between the two.' That was how Herodotus himself began his book; when he wrote, about 2,400 years ago, that was all the introduction he needed. But this one is longer, because there are some points to be mentioned which he could take for granted since they were already known to his readers, and some others which are useful if he is to be seen in the light of what has happened since.

The world in Herodotus' time

Herodotus lived in the fifth century before Christ; no one knows his dates exactly, but about 484–430 B.C. seems likeliest. This means that he was a boy at the time of the Persian Wars, which he took as the main theme of his book. Halicarnassus, his home town, was in what is now Turkey. Then, it was a largely Greek city, probably in origin a settlement from the mainland of Greece. During the years up till about 1000 B.C. successive waves of people speaking different forms of Greek had migrated from somewhere in the North down into what we now call Greece and settled there, driving out or conquering many of the descendants of the earlier peoples who had settled there before them. Those who were driven out from mainland Greece, or who wanted better land to cultivate, moved out eastwards across the Aegean sea and settled again either in its many islands or on its far coast in Asia Minor, the area which the Greeks called Ionia. That is how Halicarnassus came to have its Greek population.

When these settlements grew and prospered, they often used to reduce their excess population and increase their trade by sending out parties of colonists to found new cities elsewhere. So it was that in Herodotus' time the Greeks did not yet think of themselves as a single nation, as they are now, but lived in perhaps two hundred separate 'city-states'. Most of these were in mainland Greece, but many others were scattered along the coasts from Malaga in southern Spain as far east as Trabzon on the southern Black Sea coast in far eastern Turkey, and from Cyrene in Libya northwards as far as Olbia near the mouth of the Dnieper in Russia. In particular there were many grouped together in Sicily and southern Italy, and (like Halicarnassus) down the coast of Asia Minor.

Some colonies might remain subject to their mother city, but otherwise all these 'city-states' were independent nations. Most of them consisted of a single town, with the countryside and villages round it. The average size was about the same as that of an English county, and none of them had a population of more than half a million at the largest; most of them had far less. Yet each had its own laws, its own government, its own army consisting mostly of its own citizens, its own currency, weights, and measures, quite often even its own way of reckoning dates, and its own way of talking, or 'dialect'; but there were recognizable groups that shared similar dialects, such as the Ionians (who included Athens but otherwise mostly the Aegean islands and the cities of Asia Minor) and the Dorians (who included Sparta and most of the rest of the Peloponnese). The Ionians had been one of the earlier waves of migration into Greece and had largely been driven out by the Dorians, who arrived later.

These scattered Greek cities were often threatened by enemies, either other Greeks, still land-hungry, or hostile natives. This meant that war was very much part of almost every Greek's way of life. It also meant that Greeks developed a strong awareness of what they had in common, their 'Greekness'. However much one Greek city might quarrel with another, as they often did, and however much Dorians might despise Ionians for being soft, or Ionians laugh at Dorians for being good at nothing but fighting, they could at least understand each other—not like foreigners, whose languages all sounded to Greeks like 'bar-bar-bar' (or 'rhubarb-rhubarb-rhubarb'). So the Greek word 'barbaros' meant at first simply 'a foreigner'; it is the word translated by 'non-Greek' in Herodotus' opening paragraph quoted at the beginning of this introduction.

By Herodotus' time, the word was well established, and Herodotus often used it to mean 'Persian', since the main group of foreigners who made themselves felt to the Greeks as a whole was the Persian empire. But they were certainly not a 'barbarous' nation in the modern sense, and Herodotus uses the term 'barbaros' with no disrespect; indeed his very first sentence draws attention to the fact that his history would deal with 'non-Greek' achievements as well as Greek ones, and that they were equally 'amazing'. As a result a later Greek historian even accused him of being 'philobarbaros', or 'biased in favour of Greece's enemies', though to us this broad-mindedness is one of the best things about Herodotus. In an age when his country-men were more and more coming to regard their own civiliz-ation as the only one, Herodotus wants to correct this mistake by pointing out the many glories of other civilizations. But during the fifth century B.C. Greek civilization did make such progress that they began to have some grounds for regarding other nations as inferior. As a result the word 'barbaros' gained its secondary meaning of 'uncivilized' or 'barbarous'. And it is this sense that survives in English.

Greek civilization in Herodotus' time
The years from A.D. 1830 to 1980 have seen far faster progress in knowledge than nearly any other 150-year period in history; but Greece between 580 and 430 B.C. must have felt very similar. Starting in the Greek cities of Asia Minor, brilliant thinkers had in that time imagined (without of course having the know-ledge or the techniques needed to prove them) the outlines of the theories of gravity, evolution, and atoms, had begun or im-measurably developed the sciences of geography, medicine, and physics, had more or less invented theoretical mathematics and applied their discoveries to all sorts of practical problems in measurement, navigation, and engineering. In short they had added altogether new dimensions to the human mind, revolution-izing the ideas of religion and morality in the process and making themselves the objects of much suspicion for doing so.
That same age had also produced, largely centring on Athens, an amount of talent in art, architecture, literature, and drama which has rarely been rivalled, and has been a constant source of inspiration for western civilization ever since. Herodotus' contribution to this will be seen later; before that, to under-stand his place in literature, we must consider what sort of books had been written up to that time.

Greek literature before Herodotus

The idea of writing books comes very late in the history of man. Long before that, people had developed spoken language and had come to use it not just for expressing immediate wants but also for telling stories, both as entertainment and to preserve important knowledge. For instance, if a people believed that a certain god had power to make the crops grow, it would be important for them to hand down stories about that god so that each generation would know how the god liked to be worshipped and could thus be persuaded to continue to make the crops grow on which their life depended.

Experience would show that there were special ways of telling these stories that made them more enjoyable to listen to and easier to remember. Gradually this must have developed into special rhythmic patterns and special ways of using words, which often stayed fixed for centuries even while ordinary language was changing—as it does, all the time. Eventually among some peoples this way of using language came to be quite unlike the way ordinary people spoke and by then would be recognizably what we now call 'poetry'.

In Greece, as elsewhere, 'poets' were for a long time people specially gifted and trained in reciting the traditional stories in the traditional way, though they sometimes added sections composed by themselves. Even so, they wrote nothing down, but always recited from memory. Such poetry was called 'epic', and one of the greatest epic poets, Homer—author of the Iliad and the Odyssey—was composing probably during the 8th century B.C. (for a fuller account see *Stories from Homer* in this series). By then there had been centuries of poetic tradition, and the world described in his poems was centuries older than the one in which he recited them. The Greeks looked back to that older time as a heroic age, where gods were in very close contact with men and everything seemed larger than life.

Quite separately from poetry, at first, developed the art of writing. It had been known in Greece as early as 1400 B.C. (much earlier still in, for example, Egypt), but with the collapse of the settled 'Mycenean' civilization of that time, which was the one faintly remembered in the Homeric poems, it was no longer needed: there were no more central government records of taxes or stores to keep, and no trade needing accounts; and so writing

8

was no longer used. With a new growth of trade and prosperity developing in the Greek cities of the ninth century, it began to be needed again. The shock-waves of the migrations by which the earlier civilization had been destroyed had by now been mostly absorbed, and for keeping records of new trading activities which grew up in these calmer times the Greeks borrowed a new alphabet from the Phoenicians, the leading traders of the Mediterranean world.

However it was not long before they began to use writing on a scale far greater than Phoenicians ever had, not just for accounts, inventories, and records, but for what we would call books. The Hebrews had also begun to write books at about this time, but they seem to have used the idea almost entirely for religious writings, which soon became regarded as sacred—in fact the Bible. The Greeks were different: first they wrote down their poetry and then, by the sixth century, they started to extend their written records (which included lists of kings, or winners at the Olympic Games, as well as trading accounts) into books giving family trees or the descriptions of the towns and rivers of a region. These subjects did not seem to have anything to do with the traditional stories dealt with in poetry, so it was natural to write them in the ordinary spoken language of the time—in other words, prose.

To some extent Herodotus wrote in the same sort of way as the few people before him who had written in prose: like them he takes for granted the reader's knowledge of the traditional stories as found in Homer and like them he devotes much space to descriptions of countries or family histories. However it was the differences between him and them which made his work famous and we shall deal with these in detail further on. In general these differences were: the way he planned his book on a scale much larger than theirs, including information from both sides and using the war as a unifying theme for the whole work, as he stated in his first sentence; also the way in which he gathered and handled his evidence. To see how this came about we shall first deal with what is known of his life.

Herodotus' life
He left Halicarnassus young, because of political trouble there; much of his life after that must have been spent in the travels

that made his book possible. For a time he lived on the island of Samos, which is probably why he devotes so much space to its former king, or 'tyrant', Polycrates. He had travelled over most of the Aegean and mainland Greece, perhaps as a merchant, but the most interesting journeys were his longer and more unusual ones. In the Black Sea he had been by ship all the way up the west coast, where the Scythians then lived, to the Greek city of Olbia near the mouth of the Dnieper in what is now Russia, and all the way along the south coast to Colchis, at the foot of the Caucasus. In Asia Minor he had been to Sardis and elsewhere; across modern Syria and Iraq he had travelled to the River Euphrates, and possibly down it as far as Babylon and Susa; he had traversed the Palestinian coast, including Tyre (now in Lebanon); in Egypt he had been up the River Nile from the delta to somewhere near Aswan, exploring the pyramids and a good deal else on the way; further west on the North African coast he had been to Cyrene; and his knowledge of the Greek cities of Sicily and South Italy included living for a time at Thurii, a colony near the modern Taranto, founded under Athenian leadership in 443 B.C.

He had also lived for a time at Athens, and it seems that it made a considerable impression on him, and he on the city. He admires the Athenians for saving Greece from Persia at Marathon almost unaided, although he does not allow his admiration to prevent him from recording discreditable things about Athens too; and they, for their part, are said to have rewarded him with a huge fortune—perhaps too large to be true. Certainly he must have given some public lectures there, or readings from the first drafts of his book, because passages in it (for instance, the part about the Persians' way of celebrating their birthday party on page 27) are laughed at in Athenian comedies of the period; and to be worth putting into a comedy in the hopes of getting a laugh, they must have been at least moderately well known. It is worth adding that most people in the ancient world would have first 'read' Herodotus by listening to public readings given by the author himself—and most of them would never meet his work in any other way. In that sense he was a professional entertainer, and since this was a rare chance for learning about the world in which they lived, people were eager to hear him. But very few would have owned a *book* of his writings.

All these travels of Herodotus, given the speed of transport in those days, together with the time he spent in Samos, Athens, Egypt, and Thurii, must have lasted for years, and there is no doubt that by the end of them his main purpose was not to trade but to find out about the civilizations of the places he visited. Like an earlier Greek traveller, Odysseus (whose story Homer began by saying that Odysseus had travelled much and seen the cities of many men and 'found out their minds'), Herodotus was endlessly curious about what people did and above all why they did it. Everywhere he went he would ask people, such as the priests in Egypt, the traditions of their country; and he was more interested in the fact that they believed them than in the question of whether or not the stories were true.

What is special about Herodotus
This habit of recording the 'minds of men' rather than the external facts about things like battles leads him into trouble on occasion. He saw the Persian War as the grand theme which could unify his whole work. He captures for us magnificently the feeling of his Greek contemporaries that here was an immensely significant confrontation between East and West, and that the triumph of Greece represented somehow a triumph of Greek qualities of mind and will and freedom over Persian qualities of slavish obedience and over sheer wealth and power; and that is how our civilization has looked at it ever since. Yet in the great battles at the climax of the campaign he still lets his interest in individual stories of heroism or treachery on the battlefield (see pages 97 ff.) completely outweigh the importance of carefully recorded facts, which to a modern historian are so essential; and this makes it impossible for us to find out at all clearly what actually happened or how large the armies really were (see page 107 ff.) He is also much too inclined, for modern taste, to see the gods at work in history, and is also accused of being too ready to believe the stories he records. This he did several times try to guard himself against; a key sentence to remember is: 'My job is to report what people say, not to believe it all; and this principle is meant to apply to my whole work'. Even so, he does sometimes seem altogether too credulous, as well as mistaken on occasion; these faults were pointed out acidly by the next great Greek historian, Thucydides, just

as Herodotus himself had pointed out faults in his predecessors. Nevertheless, it is Herodotus, not Thucydides, and not any of the earlier prose writers, who has been called 'the Father of History'. The main reason for this was his new idea of putting all his various kinds of information into a book larger than any Greek prose book before it, and making it all serve the main theme; not just 'The Persian War' but 'to explain *why* there was a war'. It is this attempt to trace *causes* which was the really new thing, and which has remained essential to history ever since, though naturally later historians were often better at doing it than Herodotus was.

The other main claim he has to the title of 'Father of History' is that he does begin at times to sort out the value of his various sources. Instead of always giving one simple account, he often gives first one account, and then a contradictory one told him by a different source (for instance, in the story of Salmoxis, page 79) without deciding which is right. At other times he does give a decided view of his own (for example, on the diver at Artemisium, page 114), sometimes accompanied by the reasoning which led him to his conclusion (as in his account of the Nile floods, page 63, where he actually dismisses contemptuously the cause of its flooding which we now know to be correct and replaces it with his own view, which is wrong). But what is important is not so much that he has made a mistake, often because of lack of scientific facts or even sometimes lack of imagination, as that he is the first writer known to us to use this basic historical method of trying to choose by reasoning and logic between rival explanations and facts—to seek out what really happened. This is the real significance of his title 'Father of History'.

He is also, as it happens, a masterly teller of stories who knows how to sketch in characters, how to raise a laugh, how to keep his readers in suspense, and how to move them deeply. Above all he was fascinated by people.

These are the qualities which make him still worth reading two and a half thousand years later.

Summary of the work

As we have said, the whole work has a unity; however often it digresses, the author never loses sight of the main objective which is to describe the 'amazing achievements of the non-Greek side as well as the Greek, and in particular to explain *why* there was a war between the two'.

Croesus, king of Lydia, he tells us, was the first 'barbarian' to come into direct contact with the Greeks, partly by conquering them, partly by making alliances with them. Having absorbed by conquest the Greeks of the Aegean coast (Ionians) he dared to attack Persia and was beaten and so his empire, including the Ionians, came under Persian sovereignty. Mention of Lydia allows Herodotus to describe its past history; mention of Persia leads him into an account of Persia's rise to imperial power. Since the conquest of Lydia is only one example of Persian expansion, he gives us others (e.g. Egypt, complete with a full account of its customs and traditions, and Scythia) and these again lead to further digressions. But ultimately he returns triumphantly to the main story with an account of the revolt of the Ionians—helped by the Athenians—and this leads to the Persian decision that the Greeks are a nuisance and must be punished. And thus we come to the great invasions which are the climax of the story: and all the time the enormous power and resources of the Persian empire are brought more and more forcibly to our imaginations till we feel something of the awe which the original Greeks felt when faced with the approach of the invaders, and something of the huge excitement which they felt when they defeated them.

Finally behind the work, giving it an additional unity, is Herodotus' profound sense that Fate is at work, Fate which rules the world and men's lives, even though men often fail to see its plans, despite the help of oracles, prophecies, and hints of every kind. And when he does see, Man still has the freedom to choose the wrong course, but if he does, it is certain that ultimately he will pay the penalty. Ultimately the will of Fate prevails. So it was with Xerxes the Great King of Persia: ambition drove him on; arrogance made him go too far; he failed to heed the ample warnings of the gods, the agents of Fate, and finally he too paid the penalty.

DATES B.C.	GREECE	PERSIA	OTHER PLACES
2700 c.			Cheops
1240 c.	Sack of Troy	Rise of Assyria	Rhampsinitus (Rameses III)
776	First Olympic games		
700			Rise of Lydia
675		Rise of Media	
672			Assyria conquers Egypt
645			Egypt freed
625	Periander tyrant of Corinth (d.585)	Rise of Babylon	
612		Nineveh (Assyria) falls to Babylon	
610	Thrasybulus tyrant of Miletus		
609			Necho II king of Egypt (d.593)
600	Cleisthenes tyrant of Sicyon		
594	Solon		
585		Astyages king of Media (d.550)	
569			Amasis king of Egypt (d.525)
560	Megacles the Alcmaeonid fl.	Croesus king of Lydia (d.546)	
550		Cyrus king of Persia (d.529)	
546		Cyrus defeats Croesus	
540	Polycrates tyrant of Samos (d.522)		
539		Cyrus captures Babylon	
529		Cambyses king of Persia (d.521)	Cyrus invades Massagetans
528	Themistocles born (d.462)		
525			Cambyses conquers Egypt
521		Darius I king of Persia	
519	Cleomenes king of Sparta		
512			Darius invades Scythia
508	Cleisthenes the Alcmaeonid reforms at Athens		
500	Aristagoras of Miletus fl.		
500-94	Ionian Revolt		
498	Sack of Sardis		
490	Marathon **Herodotus born**	Death of Darius	
485		Xerxes king of Persia (d.464)	
480	Thermopylae Artemisium Salamis		
479	Plataea		

The Ancient World

1

Herodotus begins his book by discussing the reasons for the war between the Greeks and Persians. This geographical section comes in the middle of his work but we have put it at the beginning to set the scene for the stories that follow. It is noticeable immediately that Herodotus questions things that other people had taken for granted.

The Geography of Europe, Asia, and Libya

It makes me laugh to see that not one of all the people who have drawn maps of the world so far has explained the actual facts sensibly. They put 'Ocean' flowing like a river all round the land. This they show as completely circular, as if it had been marked out with compasses; and they make Asia the same size as Europe. Let me now briefly describe what size each of them really is, and how they should be drawn.

Persia extends to the sea in the south, which is called the 'Red Sea'. North of Persia is Media, then Saspiria, and then Colchis, which extends northward to the sea into which runs the river Phasis. Thus there is a line of four countries from one sea to the other. The coastline to the west of these has two large projections jutting out, which I shall now describe.

One of the projections has its northern shore running along the Pontus and the Hellespont, reaching the Aegean at Sigeum in the Troad, and its southern shore from the Myriandic gulf, adjoining Phoenicia, to the Aegean at Cape Triopium. This projection is inhabited by thirty nations. The other extends from Persia in the direction of the Red Sea and contains successively Persia, Assyria, and Arabia and ends (or rather is generally thought to end, since it actually goes on) at the Arabian Gulf, into which Darius cut a canal from the Nile. And after a large level area from Persia to Phoenicia, the Mediterranean coast of this projection runs along through Palestinian Syria and Egypt; this is where Asia ends. On this second projection there are only three nations.

All the above, as far east as Persia, comprises western Asia. The eastern part—on the far side of the line Persia-Media-Saspiria-Colchis—is bounded on the south by the Red Sea, and on the north by the Caspian, and the river Araxes, which flows east. Inhabited Asia extends as far as India; from there on it is uninhabited, and no one has any information about it.

So much for the size and shape of Asia. Libya is in the second of the two projections; it starts from Egypt. At Egypt this projection is narrow, being only about 1,000 stades (i.e. about 115 miles) across, but after this narrow point the projection known as Libya is very broad. This is why I am surprised at the usual separation into Libya, Asia, and Europe, as if they were equally divided continents. In fact the differences between them are considerable, since Europe from east to west extends along both the others together, and its breadth from north to south is, as I see it, beyond all comparison with theirs. The following paragraphs will illustrate this.

Libya's southward extent is no mystery: it is bounded by water all round, except where it borders on Asia. The Egyptian king Necho was the first to demonstrate this, as far as we know. After he had finished digging the canal (later restored by Darius) connecting the Nile to the Arabian Gulf, he sent off some ships, manned by Phoenicians. He ordered them to sail right round the coast until they reached the Mediterranean through the Pillars of Hercules, and so came back to Egypt again. Starting from the Red Sea the Phoenicians sailed along the sea which lies to the south of Libya. Each autumn they stayed on land, sowed crops in whichever part they had reached by then, and waited till harvest; then after reaping the corn, they set sail again. After voyaging like this for over two years, they rounded the Pillars of Hercules and reached Egypt. One of the things they reported, which I personally find incredible, though not everyone agrees with me, was that while they were rounding the south of Libya they had the sun on their right.*

About Asia, too, most of the facts are known; they were discovered by Darius (see pages 51 ff.). Wanting to find out where the river Indus (the only other river besides the Nile which contains

* Herodotus obviously did not know about the relationship between the course of the sun and the equator, nor about the existence of a southern hemisphere. This story, which he scorns, about the explorers having the sun on their right while sailing west is in fact rather strong confirmation of the truth of their account, and suggests that they had indeed circumnavigated Africa.

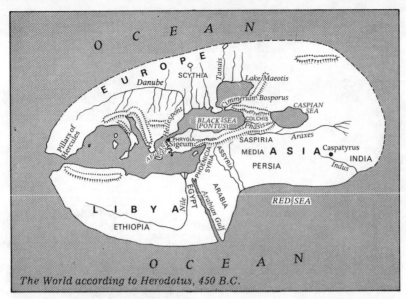

The World according to Herodotus, 450 B.C.

crocodiles) reaches the sea, he sent out some ships with people aboard whose word he could trust, notably Scylax of Caryanda. They started from the city of Caspatyrus, in the region called the Pactyic, and sailed downriver eastwards to the coast. Then, after a westward sea voyage of more than twenty-nine months, they reached the point from which King Necho had sent off the Phoenicians on their circumnavigation of Libya. After the success of this voyage, Darius conquered India and opened up the sea between there and Egypt.

Asia, therefore, has known and limited boundaries just like Libya except to the east; but as for Europe, of course, no one knows whether it is bounded by water either to the north or to the east. However, as its length is known to be equal to that of the other two together, the map-makers are wrong.

Another thing I cannot explain is why, when the whole thing is one single land-mass, it has been given three distinct names (women's names, incidentally, too); nor why the dividing lines chosen have been the Phasis in Colchis (or, according to others, the Tanais which flows into Lake Maeotis, and the Cimmerian Bosporus), and the Nile in Egypt. Nor do I know who first made the divisions, nor why they have those particular names. However, there is no point in further discussion; I shall continue to use the accepted terms.

17

Near Persepolis, on the southern side of the Iranian Plateau, in the heartland of Persia. It is a high desert region across which ran the ancient lines of communication from the Near and Middle East to the Indus and Ganges valleys. Persia, always a land power, seems to have regarded the seas that bounded her to north and south as barriers, not outlets. But to the Greeks the sea was the natural means of transport, communication, and expansion.

The Rise of Persia

2

The first cause of the Persian War, according to Herodotus, was the struggle that developed between Croesus, King of Lydia, and the Greeks of the Ionian coast.

The kingdom of Lydia occupied the area which is now modern Turkey. It had steadily expanded, conquering its various neighbours, until finally it ruled even the Greek cities on the Aegean coast. This coastal area the Greeks called Ionia and its Greek inhabitants Ionians. An appeal for help from the Ionians to other Greeks was bound to be sympathetically considered because the Greeks—especially the Athenians—thought of the Ionians as their own kith and kin.

The other dominant power in the Middle East was Media. It was ruled by King Astyages who had married his daughter, Mandane, to Cambyses, a nobleman of one of his subject kingdoms (Persia). They had a son, Cyrus, who in due course seized the Persian throne and then led a revolt of the Persians against their overlords, the Medes. Having defeated them and absorbed their kingdom into Persia, Cyrus was ready for further expansion—and so he turned his attention to Croesus' kingdom of Lydia to the north-west. He attacked it and finally conquered it and this gave him control of Croesus' subjects, including of course, the Ionians.

When these Ionians revolted (see page 95) they appealed for help to the Greeks of the mainland, including the Athenians, who readily gave it. And it was the intervention of these Greeks that finally provoked Persia into attempting to punish them in the two invasions usually known as the Persian Wars. The first invasion was repulsed at the battle of Marathon (490 B.C.); the second was larger and much better equipped, and when it was launched in 480 B.C. it was the climax of a struggle of the West against the East. What happened in this struggle is the subject of the last section of this book.

Thanks to its conquest of Lydia, Persia was one of the two most important countries in this struggle between East and West and so Cyrus is one of the key figures, obviously. Therefore Herodotus takes plenty of time to fill in the background and to tell us all he knows about King Cyrus and his country. He starts with Cyrus' early life, showing us at the same time how fond he is of gruesome stories.

The Childhood of Cyrus

King Astyages had a daughter called Mandane. One day he dreamed that she was peeing all over his chief city and flooding the whole of Asia. When he consulted the Magi, who interpreted dreams, their explanation of it frightened him; and so, when Mandane was old enough to marry, instead of choosing a husband for her from the Medes of his own class, he married her to a quiet Persian called Cambyses. This man came from a good family but was still far inferior, in the eyes of Astyages, to any Mede, even an undistinguished one.

During the first year of their marriage Astyages had another dream, this time that a vine was growing from between Mandane's legs and overshadowing the whole of Asia. Another consultation with the Magi was enough to make him send for Mandane from Persia, so that he could keep an eye on her. She was pregnant at the time, and his plan was to kill the baby at birth, because, according to the Magi, the dream meant that his grandson was going to be king instead of himself.

So, when the boy, Cyrus, was born, Astyages sent for his right-hand man, Harpagus, a member of the Median royal family like himself, and a most reliable person. 'Harpagus,' he said, 'I have something for you to do. Whatever it is you must do exactly what I say and keep quiet about it. If you prefer to serve others by cheating me you will be caught in your own trap. Take Mandane's new baby home with you and kill it. Bury it any way you like.'

'Your majesty,' said Harpagus, 'you have never had any reason to find fault with me so far, and I shall take care to see you never will. If this is what you want done, I must see that your orders are carried out.'

So he took the baby, which was already dressed in grave-clothes, and went home in tears. 'What are you going to do?', asked his wife, when he told her what Astyages had said. 'Not what he told me to do, anyway', said Harpagus. 'He's out of his mind. But even if he were twice as mad, I wouldn't have anything to do with this idea of his. What! Kill this baby for him? How could I? It's my own cousin, for one thing; and for another, Astyages hasn't any sons of his own, and he's getting old. Suppose he dies, and Mandane succeeds him; then where would I be after murdering the queen's own son? It would be fatal for me. However, the child must be killed; it's too risky to disobey; but I can't let any of *my* servants do the job—it's got to be one belonging to Astyages.'

With that he sent for one of Astyages' cattle-drovers, a man whose area, he knew, covered exactly the right kind of mountainous pasture-land, infested with wild animals. Mitradates was his name, and the woman he lived with was a fellow slave, whose Median name Spaco means 'bitch'. When this man appeared, in answer to his urgent summons, Harpagus said to him: 'Orders from King Astyages! You are to take this baby and leave it in the loneliest place you can think of in the mountains, where it will die straight away. My orders are to tell you that if you keep it alive instead, you will die an extremely unpleasant death. I am to inspect the body myself afterwards.' Mitradates took the baby and went home the way he had come.

Now his wife had been expecting a baby, too, and it happened to be born while he was away in town. What with her pregnancy and Harpagus' summons, they had both been worrying about each other, and Spaco even feared she might never see her husband again. So when he did come back after all, he was hardly in at the door before she was asking him why Harpagus had sent for him in such a hurry.

'Spaco,' he said, 'I wish I'd never seen what I saw there, nor ever heard about it either. A terrible thing has happened to the royal family. When I got to Harpagus' house, there they all were, crying their hearts out. I just couldn't understand it at all. Then the minute I went into the room I saw a baby there, kicking and screaming. Lovely clothes it had on, too, and gold ornaments. When Harpagus saw me, he told me to take it away at once to the wildest bit of the hills and leave it there. "Orders from Astyages", he said, and made all kinds of threats if I didn't do what I was told. So I took it and went. I thought it must belong to someone in Harpagus' own household, but I never guessed where it really came from, though I must admit I was puzzled by the rich clothes and the gold, and the way everyone in the place was behaving. But then one of the servants came to see me out of the city, and told me all about it on the way. "It's Mandane's baby", he says, "and Cambyses'; and it's her father Astyages who is having it killed." And here it is', he said, uncovering the baby's face and showing it to her.

Spaco took one look at this lovely, big baby and burst into tears, going down on her knees to beg her husband, whatever he did, not to kill it. 'It's no use', he said; 'I've got to do it. Harpagus will be sending spies round to inspect, and if they find I haven't killed it, I shall be tortured to death.'

Seeing that she was not going to change his mind, Spaco said: 'Well then, if I can't persuade you to save it because you must have a dead baby for them to see, here's another plan: I've just had my baby too, but it was still-born. Take that and leave it out instead, and we can bring up the princess's little boy as if it was our own. That way we'll have done the best we can for ourselves: you won't be caught disobeying orders, our dead baby will have a royal burial, and the live one won't be killed.' Mitradates thought that this was an excellent solution and did exactly what she said, putting the dead baby out in the other's clothes and cradle in the loneliest spot on the mountains, while his wife took charge of the live one. Two days later Mitradates left one of the under-herdsmen on duty and went back to Harpagus to report that he was ready to exhibit the baby's dead body. Harpagus sent the most reliable members of his personal guard, and had the body inspected and buried by them; meanwhile Spaco gave the surviving baby a name—not Cyrus, of course—and brought him up.

His true identity came out when he was ten. He was playing in the street with the other boys of the village where the herds which Mitradates looked after were kept. The others chose him, as part of their game, to be their king. He gave them all jobs to do, some as builders, others as his bodyguard, or as Prime Minister, or Lord Chamberlain, and so on. However, one of the boys in the game would not do what he was told. He was the son of Artembares, a very important man in Media, and he tried to get the others to put Cyrus under arrest. This was the way things were going when Cyrus went for the other boy with a whip and gave him a good beating. The boy was blazing with anger because he thought that Cyrus, a cattle-drover's son, had no business to treat him like that. The moment he was released, he went crying back to town to complain to his father about it (not, of course, using the name Cyrus).

Artembares, in a rage, went off straight away with his son to see the king, protesting that this was intolerable. He showed Astyages the state of his son's shoulders, and said: 'Look, Your Majesty; a slave of yours did that—one of your cattle-drover's sons. It's an outrage to my family.'

Astyages thought very highly of Artembares and could not let his son be treated like this, so he sent for the culprit, who duly came, accompanied by his father. When they reached him, Astyages looked at Cyrus and said: 'Who do you think you are, behaving in that disgraceful way to this boy here? How dare you! Do you know who his father is?'

'Sir,' said Cyrus, 'it was fair. He was with the boys in the village; we were playing and they made me king because they thought I would be best at it. They all did what I told them, except him; he just took no notice, so he only got what he deserved. If you think I should be punished for that, here I am.'

This did not sound like a slave talking, and as he spoke, it suddenly dawned on Astyages who he must be; he caught a glimpse of himself in the boy's face, and his age seemed to fit— it was ten years since he had ordered the baby to be left out to die. He was stunned, and for a long while could not utter a word. Eventually he pulled himself together. 'Artembares,' he said, 'I will deal with this so as to leave you and your son no cause for complaint. Guards, take the boy next door!' Then having got rid of Artembares so that he could question the father Mitradates privately, Astyages asked him who had given him the boy and where he had come from. 'He's my own son,' was the reply, 'and his mother's still alive at home too.' 'If you want me to force the truth out of you, you're a fool', said Astyages, signing to the guards to deal with him.

Under the torture it all came out; Mitradates began at the beginning and told the whole truth, finishing up by humbly begging for mercy. Once he had got the truth out of him, Astyages lost interest in Mitradates, holding Harpagus entirely to blame. He sent his guards off to get him and asked him how he had disposed of his daughter's baby.

Harpagus had seen Mitradates there, so he knew he was certain to be caught out if he tried to tell lies. 'Your Majesty,' he said, 'when I took the baby I thought hard how I could carry out your wishes to your satisfaction, without committing a murder against your daughter's family—your family, in fact. So I sent for this man Mitradates and gave him the baby, telling him that the orders to kill it came from you. At the same time I told him quite clearly to leave it on a lonely mountainside, and to watch it and make sure it died. I threatened him with all manner of penalties if he did not do what I said; and he did it. I saw that the baby was dead, and had it buried by the most reliable men on my staff. That is what happened, Your Majesty, and that is how the baby died.'

Harpagus' story was straightforward enough. Astyages did not show that he was furious with him for what had happened; he simply passed on to him the rest of the story as he had heard it from Mitradates, and finished up by saying: 'Well, the child's alive, and all's well that ends well. The thought of what I had done gave me no peace, and I hated being on such bad terms with Mandane. So everything has turned out for the best, after all. Please send your son over to keep my new grandson company, and come yourself to dinner this evening; I am going to hold a banquet in honour of the gods responsible for his safe return.'

Harpagus went down on his knees to the king when he heard this, and was overcome with gratitude that his disobedience had turned out all right, and that he was even being invited to a celebration dinner. He went home, and told his only son—a boy of about thirteen—to go over to the palace, and to be a good boy and do exactly what the king told him. Then, in great delight, he told his wife what had happened.

Meanwhile, at the palace, Astyages was cutting the boy's throat. He then had him butchered into separate joints, some roast, some boiled, made certain other preparations also, and waited. In due course the guests arrived, Harpagus among them, and dinner began. There were very large helpings of meat all round; Astyages and everyone else were served lamb, but Harpagus was served his own son, all but the head, hands, and feet; these were put on the table separately, in a covered dish. Astyages watched Harpagus until he had eaten enough, and then asked him how he had enjoyed the meal. 'Very much indeed, thank you', said Harpagus; and then the servants whom Astyages had trained for the part brought him that covered dish. They stood at his side, and invited him to take off the lid and help himself. He took the lid off, and saw his son's remains. He kept quite calm, however, and in complete control of himself. 'Do you know what kind of animal your meat came from, Harpagus?', asked Astyages. 'Yes', replied Harpagus; 'do as Your Majesty pleases; I am yours to command.'

With that he took what was left of the meat and went home, I

*Part of the frieze on the stairway to the Apadana (audience hall) at
Persepolis (see p. 44). The alternate Median (rounded head-dresses) and
Persian nobles symbolize the union of the two peoples by Cyrus.*

suppose to give all the remains a proper burial.

The Magi now advised Astyages that, since his dreams had been
fulfilled by Cyrus being made king in a game, he could safely let
him live—but preferably out of the way with his father Cambyses
in Persia. But Harpagus never forgot, and when Cyrus was old
enough, he sent him a message, sewn up inside a dead hare,
urging him to lead a Persian revolt against their Median overlords. The revolt was successful; Astyages was deposed (though
not before he had executed the Magi for their bad advice), but
was treated kindly by Cyrus. From that time on the Medes and
Persians were regarded by the Greeks as one nation.

Fire altars at Naqsh-i-Rustam (above), the religious centre near Persepolis. The altars date from the Achaemenid period (the name of the dynasty founded by Achaemenis about 700 B.C. and established by Cyrus) but the fire cult itself was more ancient. The priests or Magi held at the altars services which included blood sacrifices. Archaeology has shown Herodotus to be wrong when he says that the Persians 'make no temples, altars, or statues' but correct in other details such as animal sacrifice (left).

Persian Customs

At the point where Cyrus succeeded in his revolution against his grandfather, Astyages, Herodotus breaks off from his main narrative to give this general account of Persia. As usual, though some of his facts are rather unimportant, many are valuable and accurate and he seems more sure of them here than elsewhere. Indeed this concern to record factual details about foreigners is an essential part of his new approach to history.

The Persians make no temples, or altars, or statues of the gods, and regard anyone who does as a fool—I suppose because, unlike the Greeks, they do not think of the gods as having human shape. Their chief god is the sky, worshipped in mountain-top ceremonies, and they also worship the sun, moon, earth, fire, water, and winds. They worship with sacrifices, but quite unlike the Greek ones: as well as having no altar, they have no fire to burn the animal, no drink-offerings to pour on the ground, no music, no flower-and-wool wreaths to wear, and no barley grains to sprinkle. A Persian can hold a sacrifice however he likes. He just takes the animal somewhere clean, puts a small branch (usually of myrtle) in his hat, and prays—not for himself, but for the king and the whole nation (which includes himself, of course, though he is not allowed to pray for himself as an individual). Then he chops up the animal for boiling. When it is cooked, he spreads out some green fodder, preferably clover but otherwise the lushest grass he can find, and lays the joints out on it. One of the Magi must always be present at this point, and he comes up and sings the hymn which they say is called 'Birth of the Gods'. Quite soon after that the man offering the sacrifice can pick the meat up and do what he likes with it; he does not have to give any to the priest.

The really important day in everyone's calendar is his own birthday, when he has an extra large dinner. Rich people have an ox, horse, or camel roasted whole in a kiln, the poorer people have some smaller animal. They eat, as a rule, very little starchy food like bread, but their meals are spaced out by all sorts of extra courses, and that is the reason why the Persians think that

Greeks are still hungry at the end of dinner, since in Greece one never gets anything much as a second course. The Persians think that if there were any more courses, we would certainly go on eating.

They are very fond of wine, but it is not done to vomit or pee when anyone else is looking. Before discussing anything really serious it is normal for everyone to get drunk; then next morning when they have all slept it off, the man in whose house they are holding the meeting tells them the decision they took while under the influence of drink; and if it still looks right now that they are sober, it is approved; otherwise not. If they first discuss a subject when sober, then they get drunk afterwards and argue it all out again.

When two Persians meet in the street, they don't say anything, but you can tell if they are of the same class socially just by watching them; if they are, they will kiss each other on the mouth. If one is rather lower than the other on the social scale, they kiss on the cheeks; and if he is much lower, he prostrates himself at the other's feet as if praying.

They reckon they are the best nation in the world, and the further any other country is from Persia, the less they think of it; so any country which is really far away is utterly despised. This is rather like the old Median system of government, where the Medes were the ruling power but had only the countries nearest to them under their direct rule, while those countries in turn governed the next nearest, and so on.

Foreign customs catch on very quickly in Persia. For example, they liked the Median style of dress better than their own, so they adopted it; and their army uses Egyptian-type body-armour. Almost any amusement they hear about, wherever it comes from, soon becomes popular.

They all have a large number of legally married wives, but they have an even larger number of concubines as well. A 'hero' to them means not only a brave soldier; it can also mean someone who produces a lot of sons; and every year the man with the most sons wins a prize from the king. This is because they take the idea of 'safety in numbers' seriously.

A Persian boy's education, which lasts fifteen years from the age of five, is only in three subjects: riding, shooting, and telling the truth. Before that age he is looked after entirely by

*'They are very fond of wine . . .': a gold rhyton (drinking vessel) of the
fifth century B.C. representing a winged lion (symbol of the Achaemenids).*

women, and his father never sets eyes on him; this is to avoid
any distress to the father if he dies while still a baby.

Another thing I like very much is that it is illegal to put anyone
to death on just one charge, even one's own slave. This applies to
everyone in Persia without exception, from the king downwards.
What they do is to work out a balance first, to see whether the
bad things the man has done outweigh the good ones; if so, then
they can do what they like with him.

They cannot imagine that anybody could ever have killed his
own father or mother, so whenever a crime like that has actually
been committed, they maintain that the facts, if you could find
them all out, would show that he was not their real son at all.

It is illegal in Persia even to talk about anything illegal. For them the worst crime is lying, and the next is borrowing money, because they believe that once someone has started borrowing, he is certain to start lying as well.

When anyone has leprosy, if he is a Persian, he must keep out of towns and avoid all contact with the rest of the community; and if he is a foreigner they hound him out of the country: they regard it as a sign that the sufferer has sinned against the Sun. White pigeons are also driven off, for the same reason. They have a particular reverence for rivers, and no one is allowed to pee, spit, or even wash his hands in one.

A fact which Greeks notice about Persians, though Persians themselves do not, is that all their names end in *s*; search as hard as you like, you will not find a single exception to this rule. Incidentally, the names all have a meaning that refers to the owner's appearance or status.

So far all I have put down is well-established fact, but there is something else I have only heard hints about: their way of disposing of the dead. No Persian corpse is supposed to be buried until it has been picked by carrion-birds or dogs! I know for certain that this is what the Magi do, because they make no secret of it; other Persians in fact coat the corpse with wax first, and then bury it like that.

These Magi are very different from other people and from the Egyptian Priests. In Egypt religion stops a priest killing any living creature (except, of course, the animal at a sacrifice); but the Magi make it a point of honour to kill everything (short of dogs or human beings) with their own hands—ants, snakes, birds, no matter what. That is their ancient custom and they can keep to it if they please. I must pick up the thread of my story.

Croesus Encounters Solon and Cyrus

Herodotus next describes the growth of Croesus' kingdom, Lydia, and its subsequent conquest by Cyrus. But in the middle of his account he inserts a digression in which he tells the famous story of what happened when Croesus, at the height of his power, met Solon of Athens, a Greek law-giver and one of the Seven Wise Men of Antiquity.

Ultimately Croesus compelled all the Greeks on the mainland of Asia Minor (Ionia) to pay him tribute. Then he turned his attention to the islands off the coast and made plans to build a fleet with which to subdue them. When all the preliminary preparations were complete and the actual building was about to begin, a Greek arrived in Sardis, the capital of Lydia—no one is quite certain of his name—and was summoned to an interview with the king, who asked him for all the latest information on Greece. The man's answer brought the king's plans for a navy to an abrupt halt, because he reported that the islanders were planning to raise a force of 10,000 cavalry and march on Sardis. Croesus took him seriously and exclaimed, 'I wish to heaven they would!' 'Yes, your majesty,' replied the man, 'and that is just what the islanders are saying about you and your navy. They are just as keen to catch you Lydians at sea as you are to catch them on land in a cavalry battle. They want to avenge their kinsmen on the mainland whom you have enslaved.'

This brought the point home to Croesus forcibly and it seemed such good sense that he abandoned the idea of a navy and made a peace treaty instead with the men of the Ionian islands.

And so, eventually, the Lydian empire included all the countries west of the river Halys, except Lycia and Cilicia. At the height of its wealth Sardis attracted to itself all the famous Greek professional thinkers, for one reason or another. One Greek who went there was the Athenian, Solon. He had drawn up a constitution for Athens, at his countrymen's request, and then went abroad for ten years. The reason he gave for this was that he wanted to see the world, but another reason was that he did not want pressure brought to bear on him to repeal any of his laws. The point was that the Athenians had entered into a binding agreement to leave his laws untouched for ten years, and so they could not repeal them unless he was there to do it for them. However, he did want to see the world too. He visited Amasis (see p. 72) in Egypt, as well as Croesus at Sardis. From Croesus he had an invitation to the palace, followed three days later by the offer of a guided tour of the royal treasuries, with officials appointed to show him round and point out how immensely rich and prosperous Croesus was.

When Solon had taken this opportunity to have a thorough look at it all, he had to answer a question from Croesus. 'Well, Solon, we have heard a great deal here about your intelligence, and all you have learned from these travels of yours. I would be most interested to know if you have yet come across the happiest man in the world.' Croesus, of course, thought the answer would be himself, but Solon made no attempt to twist the truth to satisfy his vanity. 'Yes, Your Majesty', he said; 'a man called Tellus, at Athens.' This startled Croesus. 'And what are his qualifications?', he asked, rather sharply.

'He lived at a good time in his country's history; he had sons, who turned out well; he lived to see them all have children of their own, who all survived him; by our standards he had a perfectly adequate income to live on; and to crown all this he died a really glorious death, serving in the Athenian army at the battle of Eleusis. He was killed fighting gallantly at the moment of victory, and was given a state funeral, with a hero's burial where he fell.'

This account of all the ways in which Tellus had been happy prompted Croesus to ask who Solon would put next, thinking it certainly must be himself this time. 'Cleobis and Biton of Argos', was the reply. 'They were not poor, and they were very strong. Both won prizes at athletics and the best-known story about them is this:

'Once, at the festival of Hera, the national day at Argos, their mother wanted to go to the service. She could only get there by ox-cart, but the oxen were late being brought round from the stables out in the country. There was no time left to do anything else, so the young men got into the shafts of the cart themselves and pulled it all the way to the temple, about five miles, with their mother riding in it. All the crowds of people up for the holiday saw this feat of theirs.

'Afterwards, too, they died the finest death you could think of, which, incidentally, provided divine proof that it is better for a man to be dead than to be alive. The whole crowd was pressing round them, with the men congratulating the two on their strength, while the women were congratulating their mother on having such a fine pair of sons. She was thrilled with their success, and with the way everyone was talking about them, and she prayed in front of the statue of Hera that the goddess should grant to her sons, who were such a credit to her, the best gift that a man could have.

The actual statues of Cleobis and Biton from Delphi mentioned on page 34.
They are typical of early Greek sculpture and show the influence of
Egyptian art (see p. 69). Naked youths (kouroi) and robed girls (korai),
free-standing with one foot advanced, are the most common subjects.

'Then came the festival sacrifice and banquet, after which the two young men went to sleep in the temple—and never woke up. They simply died in their sleep. The people of Argos put up statues to them at Delphi as national heroes.'

'So all my possessions are just worthless rubbish, are they?', snapped Croesus. 'You don't think I'm even as good as these nobodies?'

'Your question left out the gods, you see', answered Solon; 'but I know them: jealous and destructive, every one of them. After all, over a man's whole lifetime so many unpleasant things happen around him, and to him. Let us say a man's lifetime is seventy years; that is, by our calendar, 25,200 days without the extra months*, or 26,250 with them; and not one of all those thousands of days turns out the same as any other. So, you see, a man is just what sheer chance makes him.

'What you are to me, Croesus, is a very rich and very powerful king. But you were asking me who was the "happiest" of men, and I am not going to award you that title until I hear that you have died without disaster. Money can help a man to get what he wants, and to cope with major tragedies when they happen to him; but there is more to being happy than money. It includes luck as well—the luck not to want what you can't get, the luck to avoid tragedies, illness, or trouble, the luck not to end up disabled, or childless, or ugly. Even a comparatively poor man with that kind of luck is better off on balance than a millionaire without it, and if his luck holds till he dies, there—and only there— is the man you are looking for: the man who really deserves to be called "happy", instead of just temporarily "lucky". Now in fact, no one has all these advantages, any more than any single country has all the natural resources it needs; so the man who I think deserves the title of "happiest", Your Majesty, is the one who has, and keeps, more of these advantages than anyone else, and whose death is not a disagreeable one. You always have to wait and see what happens in the end. God often gives a man just a glimpse of what being happy means, and then ruins him completely.'

* Ancient calendars were usually based on 12 lunar months to a year. Since this made the year too short compared with that calculated from the cycle of the sun, 3 months were added every 8 years to put things right. These 'extra months' were technically known as 'intercalary months'.

Croesus did not like this at all, and broke off the interview, entirely unimpressed by Solon. In fact, he thought Solon was an utter fool for disregarding his present success and for talking about waiting to see what happens in the end.

Some time later Croesus planned to attack Persia. Its power had been growing since Cyrus came to the throne, and Croesus saw that his own country would be added to the Persian empire, if he did not strike first. But before doing so, he tested the best-known oracles to find out which could give reliable information about the future. Delphi in Greece was the only oracle that really impressed him, so he made enormously valuable presents of gold and silver to the temple there, and then consulted it about whether he should invade Persia. The reply was that if he did he would 'destroy a great empire'. Encouraged by this, he invaded; and was defeated. In turn, Cyrus invaded Lydia and besieged the capital, Sardis.

Solon Proved Right

After a fortnight Sardis fell, and Croesus was taken prisoner. He had been king for fourteen years. In this way the prophecy came true: he did 'destroy a great empire'—his own.

They took him to Cyrus, who had a great pile of logs built like the ones used to burn corpses at funerals, and ordered Croesus, still in chains, to be put on top of it with fourteen Lydian children. Cyrus' idea may have been to dedicate the 'first-fruits' of his victory to some god or other, or perhaps to fulfil a vow; or perhaps he had heard what a religious man Croesus was and wanted to see if a god would intervene to stop him from being burnt alive. Anyhow, that is what he did. But as Croesus stood there, suddenly, even in this desperate situation, it struck him how very significant Solon's remark had been about no man being 'happy' till he was dead. Until then Croesus had not said anything at all, but at this thought he sighed deeply and groaned 'Solon, Solon, Solon!'

Cyrus heard this and sent interpreters to ask who this 'Solon' was. At first Croesus would not tell them, but under compulsion he said: 'Solon is the man I would give a fortune for every king in the world to have had a talk with.' They kept asking him to explain what he was talking about, and in the end they forced him to tell them the story of how Solon of Athens had once come and seen the splendour of his court, and had not been at all impressed. 'Everything that he said has come true', he went on; 'I am not the only person he meant his remarks to apply to, either. They are true of everyone, particularly the ones who think they are happy.'

While Croesus was telling this story the logs had already been lit. The edges of the fire were burning well by now, but when Cyrus heard the report of the interpreters, he changed his mind and ordered the fire to be put out at once and Croesus and the children taken down. It must have struck him that this man he was burning alive was only a human being like himself, and had once been just as prosperous; and that human life was so uncertain that perhaps he himself might have to pay for this action in the end. Unfortunately, though his servants tried to put out the fire, it was blazing out of control by this time, and it looked as though he was too late. However, according to the Lydians at least, Croesus saw everyone trying unsuccessfully to put out the blaze and screamed a prayer to Apollo to save him, in return for all the offerings he had made at Delphi. It had been a completely calm, clear day, but suddenly storm-clouds came from nowhere and there was a violent downpour that quenched the fire, convincing Cyrus that Croesus was a good man and had the gods on his side.

When he got down Cyrus asked him: 'Croesus, who on earth induced you to declare war on me, when we could have been friends?' 'Your Majesty', replied Croesus, 'it was my own bad luck, and your good luck. But it's the fault of Apollo, the god of the Greeks, who encouraged me to begin it. No one is mad enough to prefer war to peace. In peace young men bury their fathers, in war fathers bury their sons. Well, it was the will of the gods, I suppose.'

After this Cyrus had Croesus' fetters taken off and gave him a seat next to his own, treating him with great respect and consideration and regarding him more as a valued adviser than a prisoner of war. He told him he could have whatever he asked, and Croesus' first request was to be allowed to send to Delphi to accuse the oracle of deceiving him, and of being ungrateful for all the offerings he had made.

The answer said to have been sent back by the priestess at Delphi was that not even a god can avoid what is fated to happen: Croesus had paid the penalty for his great-great-grandfather's

Croesus on his pyre as the torches are applied. This red-figure amphora by Myson (about 500 B.C.) shows how familiar the story was long before Herodotus. Red-figure pottery, developed in Attica from about 530 B.C., proved more popular throughout the Mediterranean than the black-figure ware (see p. 86) that preceded it.

crime of murdering the king and usurping his throne. Apollo had been very anxious to put off the fall of Sardis to the next generation, but had been unable to get the Fates to agree to anything more than a three-year postponement. So at least Croesus should know that he had had three more years of freedom than he was entitled to; and furthermore, Apollo had saved him from being burnt alive. As for the prophecy, Croesus' criticisms were unjustified. All that the god had done was to say that if he declared war on Persia, he would destroy a great empire. With an answer like that, any sensible man would have sent again to ask which empire was meant, his own or that of Cyrus. So he had only himself to blame if he had misunderstood the answer and failed to ask further.

When this reply was reported to Croesus, he acknowledged that the oracle was right.

Cyrus' tomb at Pasargadae (above), briefly capital of Persia under Cambyses. 36 feet high with 7 'stages', it reflects in miniature the towers of Eastern religious architecture (see p. 49). The seal of Darius (below left) produced its impression (right) by rolling instead of stamping. The inscription in Old Persian, Elamite, and Babylonian reads: 'Darius the Great King'. Hunting and destroying lions, he represents the power and might of the Achaemenid empire under the protection of Ahuramazda, creator of the universe (shown in the sky above).

The Accession of Darius

> When Cyrus, King of Persia, died (in 529 B.C.), his son, who was called Cambyses after his grandfather, led an expedition into Egypt and in the course of the invasion went mad. At home in Persia two brothers from the class of Magi usurped power, one of them claiming to be Smerdis, the son of Cyrus. When the knowledge of this fraud leaked out, a group of seven Persian noblemen formed a conspiracy to assassinate them. They were successful.

About a week later, when things had quietened down a little, the leading conspirators held a council of war. Though many Greeks find this hard to believe, in fact they each made a speech. Otanes started by suggesting that they should now establish a democracy in Persia, and his speech went something like this: 'It is now quite intolerable for one of us to become king, since it would be so unpleasant for the rest. You all remember how Cambyses became far too arrogant and was deposed by the Magi, whom we have recently assassinated. In fact, as a ruler, he was just as bad as the Magi, as you know from personal experience. Monarchy is out of date, nowadays: you can't have someone just doing what he likes without some sort of control. Anyone would be corrupted by being in such a situation. He would begin to think he was a god and be jealous of everyone else into the bargain. It would be the beginning of the end: his arrogance would drive him to the most savage crimes, and if it didn't, his jealousy would. One would think that a king would be satisfied once he had got everything he could want; but not a bit of it, as his attitude towards his subjects shows. He can't stand the sight of any decent citizen—he prefers him dead. The only ones he likes are the really bad ones, and as for informers, he welcomes them with open arms. You can't depend on him at all: if you only treat him with proper respect, he hates you for not grovelling to him; if you grovel, he hates you for fawning upon him. But worst of all, he is the ruin of society, rapes the women, and murders the men.

You can't compare this with democracy. After all, it has the finest ideal—equality—and certainly does not produce the kind of results that monarchy does. The democratic ruler gets office by lot, he has to submit an account of his actions at the end of his term of office, and he can't take decisions without reference to the people. So that is my opinion: forget about monarchy and give power to the people. After all, they are the ones that make up the state.'

Megabazus, however, was all for letting an oligarchy take over. He agreed with Otanes' suggestion that the monarchy should be abolished, but felt that the idea of democracy was not the most satisfactory solution, since the masses were utterly useless, stupid, and lacking in self-control. To exchange the arbitrary rule of a monarch for the tyranny of an uncontrolled mob would be a case of 'out of the frying-pan into the fire'. At least a king thought about what he was doing, which was more than you could say for the people. You could hardly expect otherwise, of course, with a mob that had never learned the difference between right and wrong either at school or from its own experience. They simply rushed headlong into action like a river in spate. 'Democracy,' he exclaimed, 'let's leave that to our enemies! What we ought to do is select some of the best people in Persia (including ourselves, needless to say) and transfer the power to them. After all, the best people are bound to produce the best policy.'

Darius spoke third. 'Megabazus', he said, 'is absolutely right about the masses, but is a little confused about oligarchy. Of the three forms of government proposed in our discussion—democracy, oligarchy, and monarchy—I maintain that monarchy is by far the best. As long as your one ruler is the best ruler, you won't find anything better, will you? His rule will match his character; he will govern the people superbly; he will be much the best at keeping to himself his plans for dealing with traitors. In an oligarchy the rulers are bound to develop violent personal enmities because of the competition for public honours. Each one wants to be in charge and to have his policies carried out; the result is, first of all, ill-feeling and then a counter-revolution, with murder, bloodshed, and destruction—and, before you know where you are, you've got a dictator (in other words a monarch) all over again. And that only goes to show that monarchy is best.

'In a democracy there are bound to be abuses. As a result,

although you do not get personal enmities, you find that powerful cliques form which aim to settle things for their own advantage, and this goes on until some champion of the people emerges to put a stop to it. This makes him a popular hero and soon he ends up a monarch once again. All of which only proves my point that monarchy is best. To sum up: where did we get freedom from? From the people, an oligarchy, or a monarchy? I believe that since we were set free by a single man, this is the form of government we should establish—quite apart from the fact that we should not destroy the constitution that has served us so well in the past. Any change would be for the worse.'

These were the three views put forward, and the other four members of the council of seven supported Darius. Having failed to get his own way, Otanes, who had advocated democracy, spoke once more. 'Comrades,' he said, 'one thing is now quite clear: if there is going to be a king, it has got to be one of us, whether we draw lots or submit to election by the mass of the Persian people, or try some other method. But I am not competing—I don't want to rule or be ruled. So I am withdrawing from this competition on condition that, whichever of you is chosen, neither I nor any of my descendants have to obey him.' After that, once the other six had agreed, he withdrew. And even to this day his is the only family in Persia that is still free and acknowledges the sovereignty of the king only to the extent it chooses, as long as the members do not actually break the law. The rest then discussed how they could settle the election most fairly. They decided that they should go out to the suburbs next morning and mount their horses, and whoever's horse was the first to neigh after sunrise should be king.

Now Darius had a cunning groom called Oebares. As soon as the meeting broke up Darius went off to see him and explained the way the kingship was going to be settled. 'So if you've got any brains,' he said, 'find a way for us to win and stop the others doing so.'

'Well, if that is the way you are going to settle it,' said Oebares, 'don't worry at all; you will get the job, I promise. I've got the answer.'

'In that case, hurry up', said Darius. 'Don't waste a second; tomorrow's the day.'

And this is what Oebares did. As soon as it was night, he got hold of Darius' stallion's favourite mare, and led her out into the suburbs, and tied her up there. Then he brought the stallion out there too, and led him round the mare, nearer and nearer, and finally got him to mount her. At dawn the next morning, just as it was getting light, the six candidates turned up as arranged. They rode out to the suburbs and when they got to the spot where the mare had been tethered the previous night, Darius' stallion became very excited at the memory and neighed loudly. As soon as that happened lightning flashed from a clear sky and there was a roll of thunder. All this seemed an almost miraculous proof that Darius was the choice of heaven, and the others leapt from their horses and prostrated themselves at his feet.

The Royal Road

Persia was originally part of the empire of the Medes, but, as you have read, Cyrus conquered Media and then he gradually expanded his rule until the Persian empire finally included Lydia, Babylonia, Assyria, Syria, and Palestine (see map p. 44). He also freed the Jews from captivity in Babylon, and something of the excitement created by his activities amongst the exiled Jews can be seen in the prophets Isaiah (40–56), Haggai, and Zechariah (1–8) in the Bible. His successor, after the short reign of Cambyses, was Darius I (521–486 B.C.) and he it was that gave the new empire an efficient organization by dividing it into provinces ruled by Satraps, who were responsible to the central government but virtually kings in their own satrapies. He also reformed the country's finances, developed its commerce, and built a network of roads, of which one, the Royal Road from Sardis to Susa, is described below.

Now for a description of the Royal Road. All along it are staging-posts for the Royal Mail and admirable lodgings for travellers, and it is quite safe, since it passes only through civilized areas. The section that runs through Lydia and Phrygia is about 330 miles long, and has a string of 20 such staging-posts. On the borders of Phrygia is the river Halys, and this is the gateway to the East—literally as well as metaphorically, since there are actual gates on the road which you have to pass before you cross the river, and there is a large garrison to guard them as well. That brings you to Cappadocia, and from there to the boundaries

The 'Great King' on his throne at a royal audience—this relief sculpture of Darius I with his son Xerxes standing immediately behind him is from the Palace of Xerxes at Persepolis.

of Cilicia is about 360 miles, with 28 staging-posts *en route*. On this frontier are two sets of gates with two separate garrisons controlling them. After that it is only about 50 miles across Cilicia, which therefore only provides three stopping-points, and then you have to cross the Euphrates and enter Armenia. Here too there are frontier-guards. Armenia itself, with 15 staging-posts for a journey of just under 200 miles, has four rivers which you have to get across: first the Tigris, then two different ones both called Zabatus, and finally the Gyndes, which Cyrus once divided into 360 channels to punish it for drowning his favourite horse. After that there is Matiene (34 staging-posts; 480 miles), then Cissia (11 staging-posts; 150 miles) and then you reach another major waterway, the river Choaspes, on which stands the capital city, Susa.

That makes the grand total 111 staging-posts or lodgings and, by my calculations, just over 1500 miles from Sardis to Susa. So at an average speed of 17½ miles per day, it is a 90-day journey altogether. Add an extra 63 miles from Ephesus to Sardis, and it increases the total journey from the Aegean coast to Susa by three days.

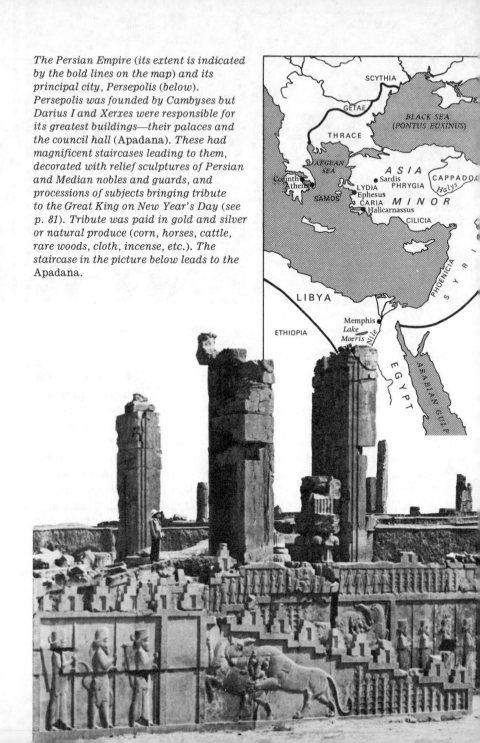

The Persian Empire (its extent is indicated by the bold lines on the map) and its principal city, Persepolis (below). Persepolis was founded by Cambyses but Darius I and Xerxes were responsible for its greatest buildings—their palaces and the council hall (Apadana). These had magnificent staircases leading to them, decorated with relief sculptures of Persian and Median nobles and guards, and processions of subjects bringing tribute to the Great King on New Year's Day (see p. 81). Tribute was paid in gold and silver or natural produce (corn, horses, cattle, rare woods, cloth, incense, etc.). The staircase in the picture below leads to the Apadana.

SCYTHIA

GETAE

BLACK SEA
(PONTUS EUXINUS)

THRACE

AEGEAN
SEA

ASIA

Corinth
Athens

Sardis

CAPPADO.

LYDIA

PHRYGIA

Halys

Ephesus

MINOR

SAMOS

CARIA

Halicarnassus

CILICIA

PHOENICIA

S
Y
R

LIBYA

Memphis
Lake
Moeris

ETHIOPIA

Nile

E
G
Y
P
T

ARABIAN GULF

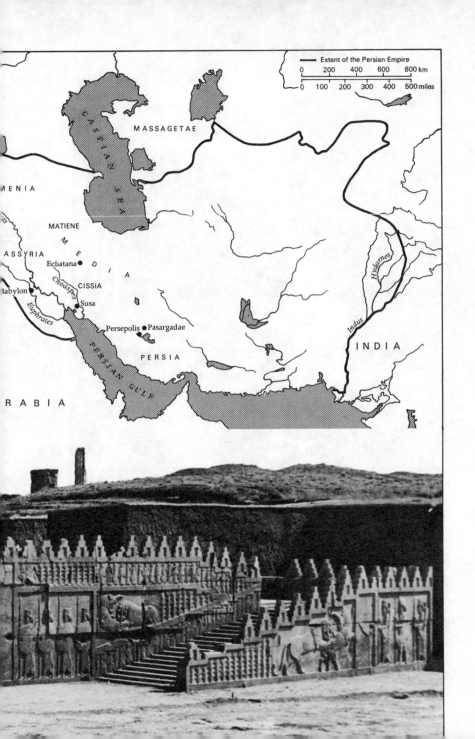

Extent of the Persian Empire

0   200   400   600   800 km
0 100 200 300 400 500 miles

MASSAGETAE

CASPIAN SEA

MENIA

MATIENE

M E D I A

ASSYRIA

Ecbatana

Babylon

Choaspes

CISSIA

Euphrates

Susa

Persepolis ● Pasargadae

PERSIA

PERSIAN GULF

RABIA

Hydarnes

Indus

INDIA

The Expansion of Persia
(1) Babylon

3

Babylon was the capital of the Middle Eastern kingdom of
Babylonia and was conquered in 538 B.C. by Cyrus. Though its
greatest days were in the past, it was still one of the most
remarkable of ancient cities. The picture (*left*) shows the Ishtar
Gate (600–550 B.C.) from a reconstruction in the Berlin Museum.
Not all that Herodotus tells us about the city is true; those who
wish to investigate the accuracy of his statements should
read How and Wells' excellent *Commentary on Herodotus*. But a
great deal is true and it makes an interesting account.

The Wonders of Ancient Babylon

Babylon is a huge, square-shaped city lying in a broad plain. It
measures 14 miles in each direction, which gives it a total
circumference of 56 miles. It was once the biggest and wealthiest
city on earth and was surrounded by a wide, deep moat fortified
on its inner bank by a wall 27 metres wide and 100 metres high.
The ancient Babylonians built this wall of brick, supplying the
raw materials for it from the clay dug out during the excavation
of the moat and using hot asphalt for mortar, with a bonding
course of reeds for every thirty courses of brick. The lips of the
moat they reinforced with stone and constructed the wall on
this foundation. On top of the wall itself they built two rows of
one-roomed guard-chambers, facing inwards, with a space wide
enough between for a four-horse chariot to drive along. In this
outer wall there were 100 gates, all made of bronze, including
the lintels and gate-posts. Through the middle of the city runs
the Euphrates, a vast, deep river with a powerful current, which
rises in Armenia and flows into the Indian Ocean. So the two
walls run right down to the water's edge on both sides before
making a right-angle and extending all along both the banks.
The city itself is laid out with its main roads running down to
the river and crossed at right-angles by side streets; and every
road, or indeed alley-way, that leads to the river has its own
bronze gate set in the wall and opening directly onto the river.
Everywhere there are grand residences, three or four storeys
high—the city is full of them. Furthermore, the wall that I have
described is really only the first line of defence. Inside is another,
hardly less formidable than the first, though not quite so thick.

Inside each half of the city, too, is another major fortification—in one, the royal palace with its own enormously powerful defences, in the other, and still standing to this day, the temple of Bel, 400 metres square with great bronze gates. This temple has an inner keep, 200 metres square, and on this is a series of towers, eight in all, each built on top of the other. You can climb up them only by a stairway round the outside, and about half-way up there are seats where climbers can rest and get their breath back. On the top of the highest tower is an enormous temple with nothing inside except a richly furnished bed and a golden table—no image of a god or anything like that. The only person allowed to spend the night there is a woman—and the god chooses her out of the whole local population as his consort. But there is a second temple lower down, where there is a vast statue of their supreme god sitting on a throne with a huge table beside him; and the whole thing, including the table and the plinth, is in solid gold—over 20 tons of it, according to the local priests. Outside there are two altars, one of gold on which only young animals are sacrificed, and a much larger one made of stone, where they burn more than 25 tons of frankincense each year at Bel's annual festival.

Among the many rulers of Babylon who were responsible for the work on the defences and temples were two women: one was Semiramis, who built the remarkable earthworks on the plain outside to stop it being flooded everywhere indiscriminately. The other queen, who reigned about 150 years later, was called Nitocris. She was much more intelligent than Semiramis and, as a result, left many more memorials of her reign, including the elaborate fortifications she put up to make the city as secure as possible against the seemingly ever-increasing and unchecked aggression of the Medes, who had taken over many cities in that area, including Nineveh.

The first thing she did was to divert the course of the Euphrates (which was originally straight and fast-flowing) into a series of channels excavated up-stream from the city. This made the river meander about so much that merchants travelling down the Euphrates from the Mediterranean find themselves passing one Assyrian village, called Ardericca, three times on consecutive days before they arrive at Babylon.

Having made these excavations she piled up the soil from the

Babylon according to modern archaeological findings. It closely resembles Herodotus' account, with bridges, citadels on both sides, and towered temples (ziggurats).

channels on either side to make the most enormous and remarkable embankments imaginable. Then a long way north of the city she proceeded to excavate a reservoir, about 49 miles round, just beside the river. The workers dug down till they reached water and piled up the excavated earth to form the embankment, reinforcing it all round with stone brought for the purpose. In this way she reduced the speed of the current by incorporating all those bends and twists, so that boats would have to take a very roundabout course to get to Babylon. Since these works lay on the direct route from Media, she thus also prevented contact with the Medes and made it difficult for them to discover what she was doing.

Among her lesser achievements was the building of a bridge across the Euphrates linking the two parts of the city and so putting an end to the tiresome business of taking a ferry each time people wanted to get across. She had all the preparatory work on the bridge done first and then diverted the river into her new reservoir which I have just described. While the main river was empty she had the bridge built and her reservoir filled, and then changed the river back again to its original course, so achieving two purposes at once.

Euphrates River Boats

At this point I think it is worth giving a brief description of the vessels which ply down the Euphrates, since, after the city itself, they are one of the most remarkable things to be seen around Babylon. They are circular in shape and made entirely of leather; the Armenians in the north cut willow branches to make a frame, but without bothering to give the boat a bow or stern, so that it looks rather like a round shield. Then they stretch a covering of animal hide over the outside to form a sort of cockleshell boat. They line the inside with reeds or straw, fill it up with merchandise (usually casks of wine), and float downstream on the current.

The crew consists of two men and a donkey—several donkeys for the bigger boats. To steer men stand at the back or the front, and pull or push on long poles. This is enough even for the largest vessels, which can take a cargo of about 130 tons. Once they have reached Babylon and discharged their cargo, they auction the reeds and willow frames, load the hides onto the donkeys, and drive back to Armenia, where they build another boat to the same design and off they go again.

River boat: on the Tigris and dated about 705 B.C., but very similar to Herodotus' description of the Euphrates boats.

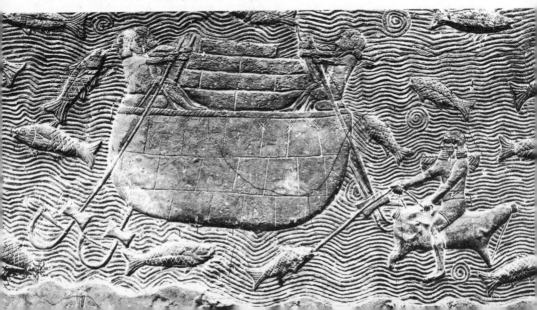

The Capture of Babylon by Cyrus

In the end Cyrus, who was later called the Great, laid siege to Babylon. He brought the whole of his army to the point where the river flows into the city and then sent a detachment round to the other side where it flows out again. He gave them strict instructions that, as soon as they saw the water level dropping to a point where they could walk in it, they were to force an entry into the city along the river-bed. Then he went off with all the camp followers and other non-combatants to Nitocris' reservoir and did exactly what she had done. He diverted the river through a channel into the reservoir, which at this time was little more than a marsh, and thus lowered the level of the main stream. As soon as they saw the level drop, the Persian soldiers made their way according to orders along the river, which was now only just above knee-high, and into the city. Even so, if the Babylonians had realized at this point what Cyrus was up to and had seen the Persians moving in, they would have made short work of them. They could have closed all the gates to the river, manned the walls along it, and caught the enemy like rats in a trap. Instead, they were themselves caught unprepared, partly, they say, because the city was so large that those at the centre had no idea that the suburbs had fallen. But that is only an excuse—in fact, as chance would have it, they were also holding a festival at the time, and were all dancing and singing and having a marvellous celebration when disaster struck. And that is how Babylon fell for the first time.

The Capture of Babylon by Darius

When Darius became king of Persia (see p. 39 ff.), a revolt in Babylon was only one of the many he had to crush before bringing his disordered empire under control. Once he had done this, he made that empire stronger than ever before, and this makes the Greek victory over Persia at Marathon (see p. 97 ff.) all the more remarkable.

When the Persian fleet was out of the way besieging the island of Samos, Babylon revolted, after making very thorough preparations for a siege. These preparations had in fact been going on for a number of years, during the period when the Magi had been in control and during the conspiracy of the Seven. In this unsettled period the Babylonians had been able to act without attracting the attention of their rulers.

But with the revolt out in the open at last, the first thing to do was to make sure that food supplies lasted. So, except for the mothers and one other woman chosen from each household to do the cooking, they rounded up and strangled every woman in the place. This news was enough to bring Darius hurrying down to Babylon at the head of his entire army to start a siege. But this did not worry the Babylonians in the least; they showed what they thought of Darius and his army by rude dances and jeering on the battlements. 'What are you Persians doing hanging about down there?', shouted one. 'Run away! You won't capture Babylon till mules have foals'—by which, of course, he meant they never would.

One year and seven months later Darius and the whole Persian army were beginning to lose patience. Darius had tried all kinds of siege engines and stratagems including the one that Cyrus had used, but the Babylonians were always too wide-awake. However, at that point something miraculous happened: a supply mule belonging to Zopyrus, whose father Megabazus had been one of the Seven who removed the Magi, produced a foal. Zopyrus refused to believe it at first, but after seeing it for himself he ordered all the eye-witnesses to keep it a complete secret, and started to do some hard thinking. That earlier remark about Babylon being captured when mules had foals now seemed very significant, and he came to the conclusion that this was a hint from heaven that Babylon was not, after all, impregnable. His next move was to see Darius and ask him if capturing Babylon was something of really prime importance to him. It was, said Darius, so Zopyrus thought again for a long time to see if he could work out a plan to capture it himself and get all the credit. Valuable services to the king are a very good way of winning promotion in Persia.

After all his reflection there was only one way he could think of, and that was to mutilate himself and turn into a deserter. Without a qualm he set about disfiguring himself in the most frightful manner, cutting off his own nose and ears, and having himself flogged and his hair viciously slashed about. Then he went again into the king's presence. The king was appalled to see one of his leading subjects in such a state. He jumped up from his throne with a shout and demanded to know what had happened and who had done it to him.

'Nobody else would have been able to do that to me but you, Your Majesty,' said Zopyrus, 'and nobody did. I did it myself. I could not bear the idea of Assyrians laughing at Persians.'

'What a dreadful thing to do! And don't call it heroic. You say you've done it to help us capture the city. You poor fool! Do you think they'll give in any quicker just because you've been hacking yourself about? You must be mad.'

'No, Your Majesty', was the reply; 'I did this without asking you, because if I had, you would have stopped me. Now it is done, we will certainly capture Babylon, as long as you play your part. I'm going over to their wall as a deserter, and I shall say it was you who did this to me. I reckon that once they've believed that they'll make me their general. That's when you must act. Exactly ten days after I have got into the city, send out one detachment of a thousand men that you don't mind losing, to the Semiramis Gate. One week later send another lot, two thousand this time, to the Nineveh Gate. Then leave a gap of twenty days and send in another four thousand to the Chaldaean Gate. None of these are to be armed with anything but their daggers. Straight after that mount a mass attack against all the gates at once but wherever your allied forces are, make sure you put the Persians themselves against the Bel and Cissian Gates. I feel sure that the Babylonians, when they see how much I have done for them, will increase my responsibility. They will even entrust to me the keys of the gates. After that, just leave it to me and the Persians.'

When he had given these instructions he set off across no-man's-land towards the enemy wall, constantly glancing back over his shoulder so as to look like a genuine deserter. The sentries on duty at the gate-tower spotted him and ran down to let him in; opening the gate a tiny crack they challenged him and finally allowed him to enter.

The guards took the 'deserter' to the city authorities, where he poured out a tale of woe. Darius (so he said) had done all this to him for plotting to start a mutiny, because the siege had begun to look hopeless. 'But he is not going to get away with treating me like this', he exclaimed. 'I've come to do you a good turn and get my own back on him. I know every detail of his strategy and plans.'

The Babylonians, seeing in front of them a high-ranking Persian with his nose and ears cut off, and covered in blood from whip-lashes, were sure that he was telling the truth and was genuinely keen to help them in every possible way. So they agreed to let him do what he wanted. He duly asked them to make him an officer, and they did.

From there on everything went according to the plan he had made with Darius. In ten days' time he went out at the head of his contingent of Babylonians, surrounded the first thousand-strong detachment, and massacred them. The Babylonians were wild with delight that he had been as good as his word and were only too ready to do anything else he asked; so when the time came for Darius to send in his two thousand, Zopyrus had a picked force of Babylonians ready to march out and massacre them as well. By now everyone in the place was talking about how brilliantly Zopyrus was doing. He waited once more for the agreed time, then marched out, surrounded and massacred the four thousand. This time there was no doubt about it: Zopyrus was infallible as far as the Babylonians were concerned, and in no time at all he was promoted to commander-in-chief, with control of the wall as well.

He showed the full extent of his cunning when Darius launched the pre-arranged simultaneous attack all round: while the Babylonians were up on the wall fighting off the attack, Zopyrus was down below throwing open the Cissian and Bel Gates and letting the Persians in. Some of the Babylonians realized what was happening and fell back for a last stand at the temple of Bel (see p. 48), but the rest all kept to their posts until they realized that they had been betrayed.

So much for the recapture of Babylon. Darius, unlike Cyrus, pulled down the whole outside wall and all the gates, and also had about three thousand prominent men impaled on pointed stakes; he did not, however, deport the rest. Not wanting them to become extinct, he provided wives to replace the ones they had strangled by transferring fifty thousand women from the neighbouring countries; and from them the present-day Baby-lonians are descended. Darius reckoned that no one else in the history of Persia (except of course Cyrus, whom all acknowledge as unique), had ever done greater service for his country than Zopyrus. He heaped rewards upon him, including annual presents of all the things which are most expensive in Persia and the tax-free governorship of Babylon for life.

The fall of Babylon, perhaps symbolized in this relief from Darius' palace at Persepolis, with the Achaemenid lion attacking the Babylonian bull.

Egypt, thanks to the 'unique climate' mentioned by Herodotus, was one of the major grain producers of the ancient world. Herodotus' account can be compared for detail with the two murals from Menena (above) and the much older figure of a woman kneading dough.

The Expansion of Persia
(2) Egypt

Before he went mad after a brief reign, Darius' predecessor Cambyses had launched an invasion of Egypt and annexed the country. This gives Herodotus the excuse for a long digression on the wonders of that country.

Some of his information is very accurate, but parts are quite misleading, since he tends to generalize about the whole country from the perhaps quite untypical things he just happened to see or hear—like any tourist who is observant but cannot speak the language and so learn the truth.

For us the main interest of these passages may lie in the light they shed on the everyday life and ideas of Herodotus' own time; from what he finds worth remarking on as normal in Egypt, it is usually easy to work out what was normal to him, and to compare that with what is now normal to us.

The Egyptians

I have a great deal to say about Egypt, since there are more remarkable things there, both natural and man-made, than in any other country, and so it is well worth the space.

The climate is unique, and the Nile is totally unlike any other river; similarly, the population has a character and way of life quite different from that of the rest of the world. In Egypt it is the women who do the buying and selling, and the men who stay at home and make the clothes. Men carry things on their heads, women on their shoulders. Women stand up to relieve themselves, men squat: and they always do it indoors, though they have their meals in the street. If you have got something unpleasant to do, they say, you should do it where people can't see you; but if it is not unpleasant, why not do it in public? No woman can enter any priesthood, either of a god or goddess; but a man can be a priest of either. Sons do not have to support their parents if they don't want to; but daughters must, whether they like it or not. All over the world priests wear their hair long; in Egypt they shave it all off. When there has been a death in the family, the sign of mourning for the close relatives, in most places, is to cut their hair short; in Egypt that is the time for letting the hair and the beard grow, though usually they keep both well trimmed.

Other people do not keep animals in the house; Egyptians do. Others use wheat and barley as their staple diet; Egyptians disapprove of anyone who does this and they make their own flour from rye—some people call it 'spelt'. Egyptians mix dough with their feet but potters' clay with their hands and they even pick up dung. They, and those who learnt it from them, are the only people to practise circumcision. It is the men who wear two garments and the women only one. Greeks write and calculate from left to right; in Egypt they go from right to left and call it 'the right way'! They have two kinds of script—hieratic for religious writings and demotic for the rest.

They take religion to the most extraordinary lengths. For instance, their mugs are made of bronze and they wash them up every day!—and they all do it, not just a few. They are particularly fussy about hygiene and always keep their clothes (which are made of linen) freshly laundered. This also explains the practice of circumcision mentioned above, since they would rather be hygienic than handsome. As for the priests, they shave all over every other day. This is to make sure that there are no lice or anything foul like that on their bodies when they carry out their religious duties. Among their countless other religious obligations, they are compelled to have a cold bath twice daily and twice nightly. But despite that the priesthood has its advantages too: free board and lodging for one thing, with bread from the temple stores, plenty of beef and goose every day, and proper wine—but no fish or beans. Beans are never grown as crops in Egypt, and no one eats the wild ones, raw or cooked. In fact priests can't so much as bear the sight of beans, because they are regarded as unclean.

Cats and Crocodiles

The Egyptians have many domestic animals and would have many more if their cats did not behave as I will describe. You see, first of all, once their kittens are born the females refuse to have anything to do with the toms. They, of course, find this rather frustrating, but they have found the perfect answer. They take the kittens away from their mothers, either openly or by stealth, and kill them off—though they don't eat them. As a result, since all cats are fond of large families, the females want more kittens and back they go to their mates again.

Then again, whenever there is a fire anywhere, the cats behave very oddly indeed. The Egyptians, who know what is going to happen, stand guard round the blazing building, making no attempt to put out the fire, but all trying to catch the cats which dodge round or leap over them and plunge into the flames —which causes the Egyptians great distress. Indeed, their cats are thought to be so special that in any household where one of them dies a natural death the members all shave their eyebrows, though when a dog dies they shave their heads and bodies as well. They have a special cat-cemetery at Bubastis where dead cats are interred after being embalmed. Dogs of all breeds, including hunters, are buried in their home towns but their graves also are treated as sacred. Fieldmice and hawks are taken to Buto and ibises to Hermopolis for burial. As for bears, which are rather rare, and wolves, which are only about the size of foxes, these are buried on the spot wherever they are found dead.

You will have heard of the crocodiles. These are their habits. They never eat during winter. They are four-footed amphibians and lay their eggs on dry land, where they also spend most of the day; but they spend the whole night in the water because it is warmer than the open air with its heavy dew. Of all the animals that I have seen, the crocodile grows the most from the smallest beginning: it develops from an egg which is only about the size of a goose's, and its young are appropriately small. Yet it grows to a length of about 8 metres. It has little piggy eyes and the most enormous teeth, some of them sticking out like fangs. But unlike any other wild animal, it has no tongue and moves its upper instead of its lower jaw. It has tremendous claws and impenetrable scales on its back. Though blind under water, its sight is otherwise very sharp, and because it spends so much of its time in the water, its mouth is full of leeches. It is shunned by bird and beast alike, except for the Egyptian plover, which is a great help to it, because whenever the crocodile leaves the water and dozes, with its mouth wide open (and usually facing west), the plover climbs into its mouth and gobbles up the leeches. The crocodile is very pleased with this kindness and so never does the bird any harm.

There are lots of ways of catching crocodiles, but I think the following is the most interesting. They fix a large hunk of pork to a huge hook and throw it out into mid-stream, and then

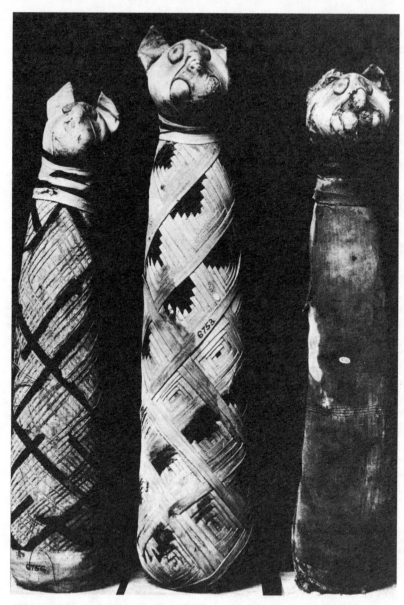

'They have a special cat cemetery . . .': a group of mummified cats, bandaged with white and dyed linen cloth. The eyes and ears are made of linen pads painted and sewn onto the outer wrappings.

stand on the bank of the river beating a live pig. The crocodile hears the squealing and, on its way to investigate, comes across the hunk of pork on the hook, and devours it. The hunter then hauls him ashore, and the first thing he does is to slap mud over the crocodile's eyes. This turns a difficult and dangerous job into a simple operation.

Medical Science and Embalming

In the cultivated part of Egypt they take a particular interest in the past. Their records go back to the beginnings of man's existence, and they know more about the subject than anyone I have ever come across.

Every month, for three days in succession, they have a thorough clean-out of their insides, using emetics and enemas. They do this for the good of their health, because they believe that all illnesses come from ordinary food. As a matter of fact, they are the healthiest people on earth, except for the Libyans, but in my opinion this is really because their climate is so consistent. Changes are what make people ill, especially weather changes. They eat rye-bread and their normal drink is beer.

Every doctor is a specialist in one single illness, and the place is full of them: eye-specialists, head-specialists, tooth-specialists, gut-specialists, and some who specialize in the kind of diseases which cannot be pinned down to any particular part of the body. There are also embalming-specialists.

When a customer brings a corpse to these embalmers, they show him realistically painted wooden models of their three different grades of mummy, ranging from the cheapest to the best quality version, which they claim represents a Being too sacred for me to mention here by name. They ask the customer which type of treatment he wants for the body; he agrees a price, and then goes away leaving them to get on with the job in their workshops. I shall describe the *de luxe* treatment first. They start by taking out the corpse's brain through the nose with a specially-shaped iron tool. (Part of the brain needs chemical treatment first). Then they cut open the side, below the ribs, with a sharp piece of flint, and take out the whole gut. They wash out the inside, and then rinse it through, first with palm-wine and then with an aromatic compound, after which they stuff it with every kind of spice, including pure crushed myrrh and cassia, but not incense, and then they stitch it all back again. After this, the body is totally immersed in an alkaline solution and pickled, or 'embalmed', for ten weeks; it must not be longer. The last stage is to wash it and wind it round all over with strips of linen, gummed on the underside (gum is used in Egypt regularly, as a substitute for glue). In this state the body is delivered back to the relatives, who shut it up in a wooden case they have made for it, shaped like a person, and put it safely away in a burial vault, leaning it upright against a wall.

The second treatment is simpler, for those who want something less expensive. The body is not cut open nor the gut removed. It is left in position and injected full of cedar-oil with a syringe; the anus is then stopped up to hold the oil in place. The ten-week pickling follows as before, after which the cedar-oil is drained off; it is so strong that by then it has dissolved the gut and all the insides, and brings them out with it. Meanwhile the flesh has been dissolved by the alkali, so all that is left is the skin and bones. The body is then returned with no further treatment. The third treatment is for the poorest customers, and consists simply of cleaning out the gut with a purgative made of radish-oil; the normal ten-week pickling follows, and the body is returned.

Burial: the mummy was returned to the relatives and escorted to its tomb. Here we see the funeral offerings heaped up outside and oil about to be poured onto them from a jar; the sorrowing wife hands the mummy to Anubis, the jackal-headed god of the dead; the inscribed tablet is dedicated to Osiris, Lord of the Underworld. The pyramidal tomb is situated among (far right) the Hills of the West.

The Nile

When the Nile overflows, it floods both its banks to an average distance of forty miles. But why it does so I find it impossible to discover either from the religious authorities or from anyone else. I would particularly like to know why it starts flooding in mid-summer, of all times, and goes on doing so for over three months before sinking back to its original level, where it stays till the next mid-summer. This is precisely the opposite of what any normal river does, and no one in Egypt has any idea of why it happens. It is also the only river not to produce a breeze, and I would like to know the reason for that too.

Now there are always Greeks around who want to make a name for themselves for intelligence. They offer three explanations, two of them not worth mentioning, except in outline. The first is that the prevailing summer winds in the Mediterranean blow from the north and prevent the river from discharging into the sea. Yet the frequent failure of these winds to blow at the appropriate season has never stopped the Nile flooding as usual. And furthermore, if these winds really were responsible, they would certainly have the same effect on other north-flowing rivers— particularly since these are all smaller than the Nile and the pressure of their currents correspondingly weaker. Yet though there are many such rivers in Syria and Libya, none of them behaves like the Nile.

The second theory is still less scientific and seems more like something out of a children's story-book. This suggests that there is a river called Ocean which runs all the way round the world, and that the whole reason for the Nile rising as it does is because it flows out of the river Ocean. Of course this cannot actually be disproved, since there are no facts to test it by. But no river of that name exists as far as I know, and I can only imagine that Homer or one of the early poets invented it and put it into one of his works.

The third theory—that the Nile is swollen by melting snow—is much more plausible and much the most mistaken. It is a blind refusal to face the facts. After all, the Nile flows from Libya and through the middle of Ethiopia (both of which are very hot indeed) and then into Egypt, which is much cooler. So any sensible person would realize that snow is not the reason: after all, the winds from that region are hot, there is no rain or snow there, and since rain always comes within five days of a snowfall, if snow ever did fall there, it would be bound to rain as well—which it does not. In actual fact it is so hot that the natives are burnt black by the sun, kites and swallows live there all the year round, and cranes migrate there to avoid the cold northern winters. Yet those are the very same areas where the Nile rises and through which it passes. If there was even the smallest amount of snow there, these characteristics which I have described could not possibly occur.

I suppose that, having criticized the theories of everyone else, I must now produce my own, even though the subject seems impossibly obscure. Well, to put it briefly, I think that during the winter months the sun is driven off his normal course by the winter winds and takes a more southerly route over the hinterland of Libya. Obviously the country which the sun is nearest to, or passing over, is going to have the biggest shortage of water, and the streams which feed its rivers will dry up. So therefore, when in winter the sun passes over Libya, it has exactly the same effect as it does elsewhere in summer on its normal course. The sun, aided by the fact that Libya has permanently clear air, high temperatures, and an absence of any cold winds, sucks up water and then draws it along further south until it is caught and vaporized by the winds there. You will notice that the winds from that region—namely, south and south-westerlies—are much the wettest, and this bears out my theory. When the winter weather further north moderates, the sun returns to his normal route across the heavens, and so once more absorbs water from all the rivers alike. As a result, in winter every river except the Nile rises considerably, because the rainy weather turns every gully in the country into a torrent; but in summer the rains cease, their water is once more absorbed by the sun, and the rivers sink to a trickle.

But the Nile is the opposite. It has no rain to swell it in winter: its waters are being sucked up by the sun which is now in the far south. And so, unlike any other river, it alone runs much lower in winter than in summer, because in summer its rate of evaporation is the same as that of any other river in Egypt, but in winter its evaporation-rate is much higher by comparison, because the sun is so much nearer. To summarize: in winter other rivers *rise* from their normal summer level; in winter the Nile *falls* from its normal summer flood, because at that time of year the sun's evaporating effects are being felt in the far south, where only the Nile rises.

Now for the course of the Nile. We know about this for a considerable distance beyond the boundaries of Egypt, in fact for about a thousand miles. Beyond that no one can say very much for certain, since the land is a sun baked desert. But I did pick up a story concerning its source from some Nasamonians at about third hand. They said that the sons of some of their chiefs had a number of wild escapades when they were young, and that one of the crazy things they did was to draw lots for five of their group to go and explore the Libyan desert and try to find out more about it than had been discovered hitherto. The chosen five were duly sent out by their friends, well equipped with water and food. They left civilization behind and then even the areas inhabited only by wild animals, and headed out west across the desert. After travelling across nothing but sand for weeks on end, at long last they saw trees growing out in the open desert. They went up to them, but the moment they started to pick the fruit growing there, they were set upon by tiny men, about four feet high, who took them prisoner and carried them off. Neither party understood the other, but the pygmies led them across an enormous swamp till they came to a city where all the inhabitants were the same size as their captors and all had black skins. A vast river, full of crocodiles, ran due east past this city.

The rest of the story merely states that these adventurers got safe home again and that the people whose country they reached were all magicians. But it seems reasonably likely that the river must have been the Nile, since we know that it has crocodiles and does flow from Libya and cuts that country in two. I myself am inclined to deduce that it is the same length as the Danube to which its course is parallel, though at opposite sides of the world.*

* See map on page 17 for Herodotus' idea of the Nile's course.

The Great Pyramid of Cheops

Up to the reign of Rhampsinitus (see p. 68 ff.) Egypt is said to have enjoyed good government with admirable laws; but once Cheops succeeded him, everything went wrong. He closed all the temples, banned religious ceremonies, and then proceeded to use the Egyptians as slave labour, compelling them to collect blocks of stone from the quarries in the Arabian highlands, drag them as far as the Nile, and float them across in boats. At that point others were forced to take over and transport them to the so-called Libyan Mountains. All this involved a permanent workforce of 100,000 men operating in three-month shifts, and even so it took ten years of hard labour just to get the road built for bringing the stones along. So that alone was an enormous task, almost as bad as the building of the pyramid itself if you include the other preparations like digging the underground burial chambers for him in the hillside under the site, and diverting the Nile so that it flowed round the whole area and turned it into an island.

Then they spent another twenty years building the pyramid. It is 250 metres square at the base and 250 metres high, made of polished stone blocks, the smallest 10 metres long, and all beautifully fitted together. The pyramid was built in a series of courses or tiers, like a great staircase. First they laid the whole base and then, with a crane made of short timbers, they raised the next layer of stones onto it, thus creating the first 'step', so to speak. To get the blocks up to the third level, they used another crane, and so on with a series of cranes standing on each level raising the blocks a storey at a time. (They may, possibly, have used the same crane each time, moving it up storey by storey, since they were easily manoeuvred). They finished the top part of the building first, and then proceeded downwards, ending at ground level with the base.

There is also some record of expenses—in Egyptian—carved on the building, giving details of expenditure on radishes, onions, and garlic for the workers. My guide told me that it amounted to 1600 talents of silver (enough to give a drachma each—or two days' pay—to some ten million Athenian workers at today's prices). If that is really true, it gives one some idea of what must have been spent on tools and equipment, not to

The Pyramid of Cheops, with funerary temple in foreground

mention food and clothing, both during the building operations which I have described and also during the considerable time they must have spent quarrying and transporting the stones and excavating the underground chambers.

Cheops ran short of money. But he was such a villain that he hired out his own daughter to a brothel and gave her strict instructions what to charge—though I was not told how much that was. She did as she was told but also went into business on her own account as well. She wanted to leave some sort of memorial of herself behind, so she insisted that each of her clients should supply her with one block of building stone as an extra fee. From this, they said, she collected enough stones to build her own pyramid, 45 metres square, which you can still see to this day. It is the middle one of the three which stand in front of the great pyramid of her father, Cheops.

Rhampsinitus

Rhampsinitus was the richest king in the whole history of Egypt. None of his successors possessed nearly such a vast fortune. The story I was told about him was that he had a special stone strong-room built to keep his money safe. Now, one side of it ran along the outside wall of his palace, and the builder thought this was too good a chance to miss. So he made one of the stones movable, so that a couple of men—or possibly even one—could remove it from the wall.

Years later, long after the strong-room was finished and all the treasure stored up inside, the builder was on his deathbed. He called for his two sons and told them how he had arranged for them to have an unlimited income for life. He gave them precise measurements for finding the stone and explained exactly how to prise it out of the wall. 'Just remember all that', he said, 'and you'll be Controllers of the king's treasury.'

They wasted no time. The night after their father died they went to the palace, found the stone, and had no trouble escaping with a large haul of silver. The next time the king happened to open the strong-room, he was amazed to find that some of his money-chests were no longer full; he could not understand it, because the door-seals were still intact. This happened two or three more times and the money level kept dropping as the burglars went on with their activities. And so, eventually, the king had some man-traps made and installed round the money chests.

Once again, along came the thieves. One of them climbed into the strong-room as usual, went up to one of the chests, and promptly fell into a trap. He realized at once that this was the end of him, so he called out to his brother and explained what had happened. 'Quick!', he said, 'come in here and cut my head off. Otherwise, once they catch me and discover who I am, they will soon track you down too; and that will be the end of you.' The other saw the force of this argument at once and did not need much persuasion. He cut off his brother's head and took it back home with him, having carefully replaced the stone behind him as usual.

The next day the king went into his strong-room and was utterly amazed to find a body in the trap with no head on, while the

Karnak: the temple of Rameses III (Rhampsinitus), showing colossi of the king standing guard outside. The monumental quality of Egyptian sculpture is something very obviously transmitted to Greece—see for example the statues of Cleobis and Biton (p. 33).

place was still apparently intact with no entrance or exit hole. So he decided to hang the thief's body out over the palace wall and to station guards there with orders to arrest and bring to him anyone they observed showing signs of distress on seeing the corpse.

This action upset the thieves' mother terribly. 'I don't care how you do it,' she said to her surviving son 'but you must think of some way of getting your brother's body down from there and bringing it home. And if you don't', she added threateningly, 'I shall go straight to the king and tell him who has been stealing his money.' In fact she made her son's life quite miserable, and though he tried for a long time to talk her out of it, he met with no success. So he finally thought up the following scheme.

He harnessed some donkeys, loaded them with full wine-skins, and started to drive them along the road past the palace. When he got near the guards, he gave a sharp tug at two or three of the skins, and undid the seams where they were sewn up at the bottom. Then, as the wine started cascading out, he began to tear his hair and howl with grief, pretending to be too desperate to decide which donkey's load to try to save first. When the guards saw all this wine flowing about, they thought it was too good a chance to miss. They dashed out into the road with buckets and began to catch it as it poured out. Meanwhile the owner, in what seemed to be sheer rage, swore at them all continuously. But they kept telling him not to worry and in the end he pretended to be soothed by this and to recover his temper. Finally he drove his donkeys to the side of the road and started rearranging the skins again.

After this they all got talking, and one of the guards pulled his leg and made him laugh. So he promptly pretended to forgive them all and handed out another skin of wine, which they all settled down to drink on the spot, inviting him to stay and join the party. So he allowed them to persuade him and stayed. As one drink followed another they all became thoroughly relaxed and friendly and he gave them another skin, and then another, until eventually the guards had all drunk far too much. In fact, they could not stay awake any longer and dozed off just where they were. This was the brother's chance. It was very dark by now, so he untied the body, and then, to make the guards seem silly, he shaved off the right half of their beards (Egyptians take

Egyptian princesses: fresco from the tomb of Akhenaten

a great pride in their beards). Then he loaded the body onto the
donkeys and drove them off home, having thus carried out his
mother's orders.

The king was fearfully angry when he was told that the body
had been snatched, and the story goes—though I don't believe
it—that in his eagerness to find out at all costs who this aston-
ishingly daring criminal could be, he installed his own daughter
in a brothel, and told her to accept all customers alike, but to
make each of them first tell her the cleverest and then the
wickedest thing he had ever done. After that she was to arrest
the one who told the story of the theft, and not to let him go.

So the princess did as she was told. But when the thief heard
that she was asking all these questions, he spotted the reason
at once. So he decided he would still keep one jump ahead of the
king. He got hold of a fresh corpse and cut off one hand and arm,
which he tucked under his clothes; then he went off to pay the
princess a visit. When she asked the usual question, he answered

with the story of how he had cut off his brother's head (that was the wickedest thing), and then recovered his body (that was the cleverest). As soon as she heard this the girl grabbed at him, but of course it was dark in there and the thief just gave her the dead man's hand. She caught hold of that and clung to it thinking it was his, while he simply let go and walked out.

When the news of this third exploit reached the king, he was so impressed by the bold cunning of the man that in the end he sent a proclamation round the whole country offering an amnesty and a rich reward if the person responsible presented himself at the palace. The thief believed him and presented himself. Rhampsinitus congratulated him heartily and gave him the princess in marriage, saying that he must be the world's greatest genius. 'After all,' he said, 'Egyptians are much the most brilliant people in the world, and you are much the most brilliant Egyptian.'

Another story they told me about this king is that he went down alive into what we call 'Hades' and gambled with Demeter, the queen-mother of the underworld, and that she gave him a golden wash-basin as a souvenir.

If anyone can believe that sort of thing, let him. As far as I am concerned, my principle throughout this work is simply to write down what people in each country have told me.

Amasis, King of Egypt

Once King Apries had been deposed, Amasis became king. At first the Egyptians refused to take him seriously, since his background was undistinguished—he was a commoner from a very ordinary family. But he won their allegiance by subtlety rather than by brute force. He had innumerable treasures, including a golden foot-bath in which he and his guests used regularly to wash their feet before dinner. He ordered this to be broken up and made into a statue of some god or other, and then set it up in a suitable part of the city. The Egyptians used to make pilgrimages to it and to treat it with great reverence. When Amasis heard about this, he called the Egyptians together and explained how he had ordered the statue to be made from the foot-bath in which their fellow-Egyptians had previously peed, vomited, and washed their feet. Yet now it was an object of extreme devotion. 'And the same thing happened to me', he said, 'as to that foot-bath. I may once have been a common man of the people, but now I am your king. So you had better start treating me with the same sort of honour and respect.' And that was the way he persuaded the Egyptians to accept the fact that they were his subjects and servants.

The way he organized his affairs was interesting too. He dealt with all his business between the hours of dawn and the time when the market-place was getting full—and with great efficiency and enthusiasm. After that he drank and amused himself with various low companions, making no attempt to use his time profitably. His friends, however, did not really approve —and said so. 'You are wrong, Your Majesty,' they said, 'to indulge in such deplorable activities. You ought to sit all day in solemn state upon your throne doing important business, so that the Egyptians realize that they are ruled by a great king. This would also help to improve your public image. At present you are not behaving like a king at all.'

'Archers', replied the king, 'only string their bows when they want to use them. Then they unstring them again. If they are tense all the time, they break and are useless when needed. People are just the same. If they insist on working flat out all the time and never let themselves relax for a minute, they gradually go mad without realizing it or else have a stroke. It is because I am very well aware of this tendency that I insist on regular relaxation.'

Now all this may or may not be true, but the general opinion is that Amasis had just as frivolous an attitude to life before he ever came to the throne; he was always one for a drink or a laugh. And if he ever ran short of cash and could not afford to keep it up, he stole some more. People used to accuse him of theft on these occasions, and when he denied it they hauled him off to the nearest oracle. Sometimes he was convicted, sometimes he was not. So when he became king, he ignored the temples of those gods who had acquitted him and contributed nothing to their upkeep, refusing to go and sacrifice there since, as he thought, their oracles were wrong and therefore not worth worrying about. But those that had convicted him and given the correct answers, were the ones he took the greatest trouble to maintain, since they were clearly the abodes of gods.

The Expansion of Persia
(3) Other Countries

Other places, besides Egypt and Babylon, came into contact
with Persia, either through trade or because they were victims
of her imperial expansion. Delegates from all over the Empire
came to Persepolis to pay homage to the Great King, passing
through the Gatehouse of Xerxes (*left*), known as the 'Gate of all
Countries'. Such far-away places proved an equally fertile
source of supply for Herodotus' collection of tales and customs.

Tall Stories from the East

In the Indian desert are found the most enormous ants—bigger
than foxes, though not quite as big as dogs. The Persian king
keeps specimens in captivity at Susa and you can see them
there. These insects are just like Greek ants and, like them, live
underground and throw up ant-hills; but their hills contain
gold-dust. Needless to say the Indians organize expeditions to
collect it, and this is how they do it.

Each man takes three camels. These animals are as fast as
horses, and can carry a good deal more. Everyone knows what a
camel looks like; but you may not know that it has double-
jointed back legs with two knees and two thighs on each leg, or
that its genitals face backwards. So the hunters take these
animals—two males and one female, who travels between the
males and must have recently had a foal. They aim to make the
raid at the hottest time of the day, when the ants are underground taking a siesta. They bring small sacks with them, and
when they arrive they fill them with the golden sand and then
head for home as fast as their camels can carry them. The ants
smell them almost at once and rush off in hot pursuit, and since
they are the fastest creatures on six legs, the Indians cannot
hope to escape unless they get a good start while the ants are
still organizing themselves. But they have another trick too.
The male camels are not as fast as the females and so they soon
begin to slow down from exhaustion. The hunters cut them loose
one at a time and themselves ride on the female, who can only
think of getting back to her foal as quickly as possible, and
never eases up. As a result, the ants eat the males, the female

gets back safe to her foal, and the Indians get the gold—which keeps everybody happy.

India, then, produces gold in great quantities; but Arabia, the southernmost country in the known world, is our only source of frankincense, myrrh, cassia, cinnamon, and ladanum-gum. Except for the myrrh, all these cost the Arabs a lot of time and effort to collect. Take frankincense, for example: it grows on trees and the trees are guarded by millions of tiny, multi-coloured, flying snakes, similar to the ones that invade Egypt. The only way, therefore, the Arabs can collect the frankincense is to smoke the snakes out of the trees by burning a gum called 'storax'. Now these flying snakes may be small, but they make up in numbers for what they lack in size. The Arabians say that the whole world would be full of these snakes, and it would be impossible for men to live in it, were it not for the genius of Providence, which has so arranged things—as indeed it has for vipers—that at the very moment of reproduction the female seizes the male by the neck and does not let go till she has bitten his head off. The female too gets what she deserves for treating her husband like that—to be born at all the young inside her belly have to eat their way out; so that is the end of the female. It all helps to keep down the population of flying snakes which, for this reason, have never managed to spread beyond the boundaries of Arabia.

Then there is cinnamon. No one knows how or where it grows, except that it must be somewhere out in the back-of-beyond. But apparently gigantic birds bring dry sticks of what the Phoenicians have taught us to call cinnamon to their mud-plaster nests on the mountain crags of Arabia, which are inaccessible to man. But the Arabs are too clever for them: they cut up the carcasses of dead cattle, donkeys, and the like into huge hunks of meat, carry them into the area, and leave them lying on the ground nearby. The birds fly down, of course, to pick up the joints and carry them off to their nests. But the nests cannot take the weight of the meat and collapse. Whereupon the Arabs rush in and gather up the cinnamon-sticks.

The sheep in this part of the world are also rather remarkable. There are two sorts: the long-tailed sheep and the broad-tailed sheep. Both are unique. The broad-tailed, as its name implies, has a tail anything up to half a metre wide, while the other kind have tails at least one and a half metres long. Needless to say, if any long-tailed sheep tried to drag his tail around all by himself, he would soon develop ulcers from rubbing it over the ground. So the shepherds, who incidentally are rather good at carpentry, have constructed little wooden trolleys and they put one under the tail of each sheep and tie it there. This lightens the load and keeps the tail off the ground—altogether an admirable solution to the problem.

The Massagetans

Not all Persia's attempts at expansion were successful: Cyrus, for example, met his match in Queen Tomyris of the Massagetans, who carried out her threat to give the bloodthirsty Persian more blood than he could drink. She cut off his head on the battlefield and put it into a wineskin full of blood.

In this description of the people's way of life, Herodotus shows particular interest in the fact that they are nomadic and use no iron. They were, in fact, a Bronze Age civilization which survived into the Iron Age, which reached the Mediterranean area from the Middle East around 1000 B.C.

The Massagetans live and dress like the Scythians (see p. 78 ff.), except that they have unmounted archers and spearmen as well as mounted ones, and that they all wear *kukri*-shaped swords. The only metals they have are bronze and gold: bronze for spear-points, arrow-heads, and swords; gold for all the decorative parts on their headbands, straps, and belts. The same applies even to their horses: they use bronze for the breastplates they put on their horses' fronts, but make the bit, cheek-pieces, and bridle fittings out of gold. They do not use iron at all, or silver. In fact, these metals do not exist in their country, though gold and bronze are unlimited.

Now for something of their way of life. First as to marriage: though each man has a wife, they share them; and the Greeks are wrong to attribute this practice to the Scythians; it is the Massagetans who do it. If one of them wants a particular woman, he hangs up his quiver at the door of her covered waggon and takes her; no one interrupts.

Next, euthanasia: this incidentally, is the only time they put people to death. When someone gets very old, his family all come along one day and kill him ritually, along with a sheep or two. Then they boil up all the meat together and have a most enjoyable banquet. This is accepted by everyone as the ideal way to die. If someone dies of disease, they bury him instead, but it is very much a second best, and they feel very sorry for him that he did not live to be killed and eaten.

Next, their diet. They do not grow any crops at all. They live by hunting and fishing, and there are plenty of fish in the river Araxes. Their drink is milk.

Finally religion. The sun is the only god they worship. What they sacrifice to him is horses—the idea being to offer the fastest-moving thing on earth to the fastest-moving Being in heaven.

The Head-Hunters of Scythia

The Scythians, a nomadic people ranging mainly in the southern parts of what we know as the U.S.S.R., were famous warriors. At one time they had even set up their own rule in Egypt. Darius' attempt to annex them to the Persian Empire was defeated by the same tactics as defeated Napoleon and Hitler in their invasions of Russia: avoidance of pitched battles, when possible, until the invaders were finally starved into retreat.

The first time a Scythian kills a man he drinks his blood. After a battle he delivers all his victims' heads to the king, and anyone who fails to deliver at least one gets nothing when they share out the booty. He then scalps him as follows: he makes a cut all round just above the ears, gets hold of the hair, and gives a good shake: the scalp comes right off. Then he scrapes away the flesh with the bone from a rib of beef and works it between his fingers until it is supple and fit to be used as a sort of towel to wipe his hands on. He strings his scalps from the bridle of his horse and takes a tremendous pride in them. The man with the most 'towels' is counted the greatest hero.

They also often use the rest of the skins to make overcoats, stitching them together like their ordinary leather jackets. Or else (the victim is dead by this stage, of course) they flay the right hand, complete with finger-nails, and use it for a quiver-cover. Human hide turns out to be very thick and very clear in colour. It is, in fact, about the lightest of all hides. Often too, they take the skin off the whole body in one piece, stretch it over a wooden frame, and then put it on a horse and ride around with it.

In the case of their worst enemies they also use the skulls to make their drinking-bowls, by sawing off the tops at eyebrow level and covering the outside with rawhide. Rich people inlay the whole inside with gold as well. Sometimes they treat even members of their own clan in the same way, if they have a feud with them and have beaten them in trial by combat. (These trials are judged by the king.) To impress his more important guests with his valour, a Scythian will give them these heads to drink out of, explaining how they once belonged to members of his clan and how he beat them.

Once a year the governors of every region of Scythia distribute free wine to everyone who has killed an enemy soldier. Those who have not done so receive no wine and are not allowed to sit with the others, which is a terrible disgrace. But those who have killed a specially large number receive special treatment and are allowed to keep drinking with two cups at a time.

The Getans, Believers in Immortality

The Getans lived on and near the Black Sea coast, roughly where Rumania and Bulgaria now meet. Herodotus is obviously dubious about their belief in everlasting life, but, as usual, he is interested and does not dismiss it outright, as the Greeks were often inclined to do. In fact, this was one of the things which made it hard for the early Christians to preach successfully to any Gentiles who were used to Greek ways of thought.

The first people Darius had to conquer on his way north to the Danube were the Getans, who believe they are immortal. The other Thracians up to that point had surrendered to him without a fight, but the Getans, who are the bravest people in Thrace and have the most highly developed sense of justice, were less obliging; so he reduced the entire people to slavery outright.

Their belief is that at death they do not really die at all but go to a god called Salmoxis. Once every five years they draw lots for the honour of being sent to Salmoxis with a report of the tribe's latest requirements. This is how they send him on his way. Three spears are held up by carefully positioned men, while other men take the hands and feet of the tribe's 'messenger', swing him up, and let him go so that he comes straight down on top of the spear points. If he is killed it is regarded as a sign that everything is all right and that the god will accept him. If not, they conclude that there must be something wrong with the man himself, so they reject him as a bad character and send off someone else instead. They brief the man on the report he is to deliver—*before* death, of course.

The story I hear from Greeks who live in those parts is quite different. They claim that Salmoxis is not a god at all, merely a highly intelligent slave who once belonged to the mathematician, Pythagoras, on the island of Samos, and was later set free by him, made a lot of money, and went home to Thrace with his earnings. After being used to the Greek way of life and their more developed civilization, he found the Thracians up there excessively stupid, and their standard of living primitive, as you would expect. So (they go on) he fitted up a big room as a restaurant for the best class of clients, and over the dinners, with first-rate food and wine, he worked to convince them that they were all immortal, and that he himself, his clients, and their children, instead of dying, were all going to go somewhere where they would have a wonderful life for ever and ever.

Meanwhile all this time he had been constructing an underground chamber. Once he had finished it, he suddenly disappeared and lived down there for three whole years without anyone ever setting eyes on him. The Getans were sure he was dead and were very sorry indeed to lose him, until one day, just as suddenly, there he was back again, and they were all convinced at last.

Personally I am not over-inclined either to accept or reject this story. What I do think, though, is that Salmoxis must have lived long before Pythagoras' time, and whether he was a local Getan god, or a human being, or a completely mythical character, let us forget him and get back to the Greeks and Persians.

Tributary nations: their numbers grew as the Empire expanded. On the great eastern stairway to the Apadana at Persepolis we see (top) Arians, (middle) Babylonians, and (bottom) Lydians coming to pay homage. (c. 500 B.C.)

This frieze from the Parthenon shows the procession in honour of Athena, patron goddess of Athens. The naturalness and individuality of the figures on this page contrasts with the rigidity of the delegates from Persia's subject nations on the previous page. Although the date of this frieze (440 B.C.) is later when sculptural skills were more advanced, the difference in outlook between the two cultures is revealed by the contrasting artistic styles.

Greece

4

Finally we come to Greece, whose war with Persia is the climax of the work. Greece was not a united country but a collection of small, independent states who shared a common geographical location, language, and customs—but not much else. Occasionally some of them formed alliances, but only for a short period; and the largest of such alliances, though also one of the shortest-lived, was the one against Persia.

But the activities of this alliance will be dealt with in Part 5. First we must go back in time a little. In the sixth and seventh centuries before Christ many of the Greek States had been ruled by tyrants, a word coming from the Greek 'tyrannos', which means 'absolute ruler'. Such tyrants were not necessarily tyrannical in the modern sense of the word; often, indeed, they were benevolent rulers who gave to their states a period of stable rule in which, thanks to their patronage, there were great artistic and cultural developments, and, thanks to the security which their reigns provided, considerable economic growth.

Of the two tyrants mentioned in this chapter, Periander of Corinth ruled from about 625 B.C. and Polycrates of Samos from about 540 B.C. while the Alcmaeonids, though never tyrants, were one of the most powerful and influential families in Athens from the seventh century onwards.

Periander, Tyrant of Corinth

Periander, who succeeded his father Cypselus, the notorious and brutal tyrant of Corinth, started by being a milder ruler than his father. But after getting advice from Thrasybulus, the tyrant of Miletus, he became even more savage than Cypselus had been. He sent a messenger to Thrasybulus to ask his advice about what was the best and most stable form of constitution to ensure his city's continued prosperity. Thrasybulus did not answer but took the messenger for a walk in the country; when they came to a wheatfield, he walked through it cross-questioning the man about why he had come. And whenever he saw a particularly fine head of wheat sticking out above the rest, he chopped it off and threw it away, until he had completely ruined the best and richest part of the crop.

When his messenger returned, Periander was naturally eager to get his answer. But the man explained that Thrasybulus had not given him an answer at all, and that he could not see why Periander had bothered to send him to a man like that, who was obviously mad and went about ruining his own property—and he explained what had happened. However, Periander understood the message at once: Thrasybulus was recommending him to assassinate all the really outstanding citizens.

And from that day on Periander made life a misery for the Corinthians; whatever Cypselus had left undone in the way of murder or banishment, Periander completed.

Amongst his other crimes Periander murdered his wife Melissa, and the result of that was still further misfortune. She had given him two sons, one of them at this time seventeen, the other eighteen years old. Procles, the tyrant of Epidaurus, the boys' grandfather, invited them to stay with him after their mother's death and naturally treated them with great kindness, since they were the sons of his own daughter. Finally, at the end of their visit, while they were saying goodbye, he asked them if they knew who had murdered their mother.

The elder brother thought he must be joking, but Lycophron, the younger, was terribly upset and jumped to the conclusion that his father was the murderer. So when they got back to Corinth he avoided contact with him, refusing even to give an explanation of his behaviour. In the end Periander lost his temper and told him to get out of the house and not come back. Having thus got rid of Lycophron, Periander then asked the elder brother what their grandfather had said to make him behave like that, but was told that they had in fact been treated very kindly indeed. Having never given a thought to what Procles had said while they were leaving, he had completely forgotten the remarks about their mother's murder, and therefore did not mention it. But Periander insisted that there must be more in it than that, and that Procles must have given them some kind of hint about something. And then, after persistent questioning, the young man suddenly remembered and told his father. Periander did not yield in the least. He merely sent a message to the people with whom Lycophron was staying, ordering them to turn the boy out of the house; and wherever Lycophron went after that, his father had him expelled. Finally he issued a general proclamation to the effect that anyone who gave hospitality to the boy, or even spoke to him, would be made to pay a heavy fine to the temple treasury.

The result of all this was that no one was prepared to speak to Lycophron or even take him into this house, and Lycophron himself felt it would be wrong to endanger anyone else by deliberately breaking the ban. So he decided to grit his teeth and put up with it, and got what shelter he could by lying in the porticoes for the night. It was in one of these that Periander came across him four days later, hungry, dirty, and dishevelled. He actually felt sorry for him, forgot his fury, went up to the boy and spoke to him. 'Look here, Lycophron,' he began, 'which is better: living like this or living up at the palace and preparing to inherit my wealth and power when the time comes? You are the son of the king of Corinth; you ought to be thinking of your position and at least showing some respect for your father. Instead, all you can do is go out and live like a tramp. What is the point of rebelling like this and being so thoroughly pig-headed?

'Perhaps you have reason to suspect me of some crime or other: I don't know. But if you do, remember it is much worse for me than it is for you: I have to live with my conscience. Come on! Surely it is better to have people envying you than feeling sorry for you? You have learnt your lesson: it is not worth fighting your parents. Just come home and forget all about it.'

Lycophron's only answer to this was to point out that his father had broken his own decree by speaking to him, and that he would have to pay the fine himself. That proved to Periander that he could do nothing with his son, so he shipped him off to Corcyra to get him well out of the way.

Polycrates, Tyrant of Samos

On becoming tyrant of Samos, Polycrates made a formal alliance with Amasis, King of Egypt (see p. 72 ff.), though he had always been on friendly terms with him, exchanging presents and so on.

Polycrates' reign went well from the start, and his exploits were the talk of the Greek world. With his hundred-ship navy and his thousand archers, every raid he planned was a success.

'With his hundred-ship navy . . .': two Greek warships from an Attic black-figure cup by the potter Nicosthenes. Note the comparatively light structure, which gave manoeuvrability at the expense of strength; the heavy beak, for ramming—the normal mode of attack; the single sail for cruising downwind only, for unlike merchant ships they depended primarily on oar power and usually put into land at night.

He captured place after place in the Aegean islands and on the Ionian coast, plundering and sacking friendly cities and enemy ones indiscriminately. His idea was that his friends would be much more grateful to him if he gave them back what he had taken from them than if he had never taken it in the first place. Amasis kept his eye on Polycrates' career, and when he saw him getting more and more successful, he sent him a letter.

'Polycrates,' he wrote, 'it is always nice to hear that one's friends are doing well. But I know how jealous the gods are and I don't like the look of this good luck of yours at all. I myself would much prefer to suffer an occasional disaster, and my friends likewise, than to be lucky all the time. It is quite essential to have downs as well as ups. I have never heard of anyone being consistently lucky and not suffering terribly for it in the end. You must take action—at once. I would suggest that you think of your most valuable possession, the one it would hurt you most to lose, and that you throw it away somewhere where no one will ever be able to get at it. And whenever you have a long run of success, from now on, use the remedy I have suggested.'

It struck Polycrates on reading this that Amasis had made a thoroughly sensible suggestion, and after some thought he decided that out of all his collection the piece he would most hate to lose was one by a very famous jeweller called Theodorus, an emerald set in a gold ring. The method he devised for getting rid of it for good was to board one of his ships and order the crew to take her right out to sea; then, when they were miles from the land, he took off the ring in full view of everyone and threw it into the water.

A week or so later Polycrates had a visitor: a fisherman arrived at the palace with an enormous fish he had caught, and asked to see the king in person. When they ushered him into the king's presence he said: 'I'm a poor man, Your Majesty, as you can see; but when I caught this beauty, I just couldn't bring myself to go and sell it in the market. It's a fish fit for a king, I said to myself, and so I've brought it to the king as a present.' Polycrates was delighted, thanked the fisherman for his kind remarks and the noble present and invited him back to dinner that night to share it.

The fisherman was very impressed at being invited to dinner at the palace, and went off home. Meanwhile the servants started cutting up the fish, and there, in its gut, they found Polycrates' ring. The moment they saw it they grabbed it and rushed off in great excitement to return it to Polycrates and explain where they had found it. He felt that there must be something supernatural in this and promptly sent off a long letter to Amasis describing what he had done and what had happened as a result. Reading this story convinced Amasis that if anything is fated to happen to somebody, there is no way of avoiding it. And reckoning that a man with such a fantastic run of luck as Polycrates, who had even recovered something he had thrown away, was bound to come to a bad end, he sent a spokesman to announce that he was breaking off diplomatic relations with Samos forthwith. Amasis did not want to be friends with Polycrates any more; otherwise he would be so greatly distressed when some disaster happened to him.

In the end, after surviving innumerable battles and a revolution (during which he imprisoned every woman and child on Samos in the dockyards and threatened to set fire to them and burn them alive, if their husbands joined the rebels), Polycrates was assassinated. But by then Amasis himself was dead too.

Arion

According to the local inhabitants, and those of Lesbos too, the most amazing thing that ever happened while Periander was tyrant of Corinth, was the trip taken by Arion to Taenarum on a dolphin.

Arion was the world's leading singer at the time, and also one of the earliest known composers. He spent most of his time at Periander's court, but the story goes that on one occasion he decided to make an overseas tour in Italy and Sicily. There he made a great deal of money and had decided to return to Corinth from the port of Tarentum in South Italy.

He always felt at home among the Corinthians, so he chartered a Corinthian ship for the passage. But once they were out at sea, the crew started scheming to throw Arion overboard and keep his money. When he discovered their intentions, he tried desperately to dissuade them, even offering to let them have the money if they would let him go. But it was no use: they told him either to kill himself, so that he could have a decent burial ashore, or jump overboard at once. Seeing no way out of it, Arion asked them, as a last favour, to let him put on all his robes and sing them a farewell song on deck. When that was over, he assured them, he would kill himself.

The crew were delighted at the chance to hear the best singer in the world, so they agreed, and came back from the bows to the middle of the ship, while Arion put on his gear and got out his instrument. Then he went up on the afterdeck and sang them a religious piece. After that, dressed just as he was, he threw himself into the sea. The ship went on its way home to Corinth, but Arion, so they say, was picked up by a dolphin, which took him to Taenarum. After landing there, he made his way, still in the same clothes, to Corinth, and told the whole story. Periander did not believe him and put him under close arrest. But in the meantime he kept a sharp look-out for the ship's crew, and when they turned up he sent for them. 'Have you any news of Arion?', he asked. 'Oh, yes', they said; 'he's all right. He's in Italy; in fact, he was making a fortune in Tarentum when we left.'

At this point Arion suddenly appeared wearing just the same things as when he had jumped overboard, and they were so badly shaken by this that they broke down under further questioning and admitted everything.

Well, that is the story they tell in Corinth and Lesbos. And at Cape Taenarum there is a monument to Arion: a bronze statue, not very large, of a man riding on the back of a dolphin.

Greece

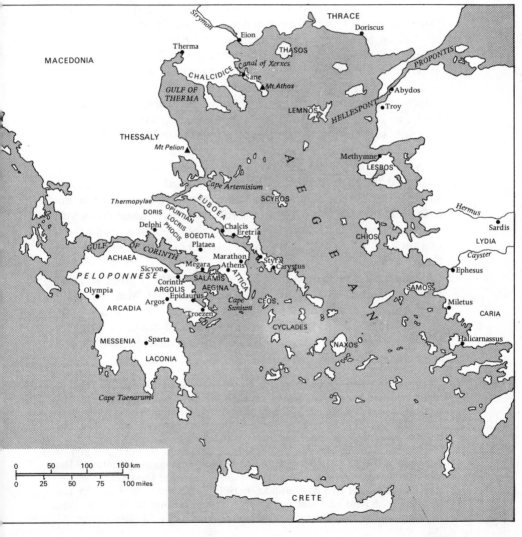

The Alcmaeonids of Athens

The Alcmaeonids had been from the very beginning one of the most distinguished families in Athens, but more so than ever from the time of Alcmaeon and Megacles. When King Croesus sent an embassy from Lydia to the Delphic oracle, it was Alcmaeon who took the ambassadors under his protection and helped them in every way he could. They, of course, reported this to Croesus who invited Alcmaeon to visit his capital, Sardis, so that he could repay him in some way for his services. When he arrived Croesus told him he could have as much gold from his treasury as he could carry away by himself on one visit. This was no ordinary offer and Alcmaeon thought about it carefully before producing the following scheme. He put on an enormous tunic, so loose-fitting that its folds formed a vast sort of pouch in front, together with the most colossal pair of thigh boots he could find. Dressed like this he followed his escort into the royal treasury. Here he dived into a heap of gold dust and wallowed in it, first stuffing his boots as full of it as he could, then filling up the folds of his tunic, sprinkling it all over his hair, and taking a huge mouthful for good measure before staggering out, scarcely able to drag one foot after the other, and looking like nothing on earth with his bursting cheeks and bulging figure.

Croesus took one look at him and went into fits of laughter, and then, as a reward for the entertainment, told him he could help himself a second time. And that was the origin of the Alcmaeonids' family fortunes, which enabled them to build up a racing stable and ultimately to win the chariot-race at the Olympic games.*

* The games themselves according to tradition were founded in 776 B.C. and were held every four years, as they still are today. Originally the contests consisted simply of running and wrestling, but later they were extended to include chariot-racing, throwing events, etc., and the chariot-race became the most important single event.
They were held in honour of Zeus, king of the gods, supreme god of Olympia, a town on the western coast of the Peloponnese which was the site of his great temple, one of the seven wonders of the ancient world. The games lasted five days and their religious purpose is shown by the fact that the first and last days were devoted largely to sacrifices and religious activities. The only prize was a wreath of wild olive leaves.

*Wrestling was always popular and in athletics contests it was the deciding
event of the Pentathlon between the two most successful competitors from
the other four events. But to the Greeks athletics was more than just
a sport: by success in the games a man won honour for his city which often
gave him a pension for life and civic honours of various kinds. And his
fellow citizens felt that he had become a living example of the heroes and
demi-gods of their folk-tales. This, perhaps, explains why athletics played
such an important part in Cleisthenes' selection procedures.*

But two generations later, when Cleisthenes was tyrant of
Sicyon, he raised the family to new pinnacles of fame throughout Greece. He had a daughter whose name was Agariste, and he
wanted to marry her to the finest nobleman in all Greece. So
during the Olympic games, in which, incidentally, he won the
four-horse chariot-race, he issued a proclamation to the effect
that any Greek who thought he was fit to be Cleisthenes' son-in-
law should apply to Sicyon within sixty days, because Cleisthenes intended to marry his daughter off within a year of the
closing date for applications. The suitors came from all over
Greece. Anyone who was proud of himself or his city joined in,
and Cleisthenes built a special stadium and wrestling arena in
which to entertain them and put them to the test.

Once the closing date for applications was passed, Cleisthenes
started his selection. He inquired into each candidate's city
and family tree, and he kept them at the palace for a whole year
testing them for courage, temperament, education, and character. He spent a lot of time chatting to each of them individually

and in groups, and he put the young ones through physical tests as well. He also had them all to dinner regularly, and this was the most important part of the test as far as Cleisthenes was concerned. All this went on for the year they were with him, and throughout the period he gave them lavish entertainment in every way. As it happened, two Athenians were the ones that took his fancy most, particularly one called Hippocleides, the son of Teisander, an outstanding candidate both for his personal qualities and his family connections.

And so at last the day came when Cleisthenes had to announce his choice and the engagement. He held a special sacrifice of a hundred cattle and invited all the suitors and the people of Sicyon to dinner that night. After dinner the suitors competed in music and impromptu speech-making. Once again, Hippocleides was the star performer and the life and soul of the party. As the drinking went on he finally asked the flute girl to play him a tune and he began to dance to it. Perhaps he thought he was creating a good impression, but Cleisthenes obviously disapproved of the whole performance. Then, after a short rest, Hippocleides shouted for someone to bring him a table, climbed onto it, and after doing some fairly conventional dances, finally stood on his head using his legs to perform the arm movements. This was too much for Cleisthenes. He had managed to keep his temper during the first table-dance routine, but by now he hated the idea of such a son-in-law; so when he saw him actually dancing upside down, he exploded. 'Hippocleides,' he shouted, 'that dance has just cost you a wife.' Back came the reply: 'I couldn't care less.' Hence, of course, the proverbial expression 'He's a Hippocleides' to describe anyone with a couldn't-care-less attitude.

So, after that, Cleisthenes gave every suitor a gift of silver for his pains and married the girl to the other Athenian, who was, as it happened, Megacles, the Alcmaeonid. And that was great publicity for the Alcmaeonid family.

Banquet scene on a fifth century B.C. red-figure bowl; festivities are clearly fairly advanced. The instrument (far right) conventionally translated 'flute' was in fact a double-piped reed instrument, rather like a pair of bagpipe chanters.

'Those Persians fight with bows and arrows and tiny spears . . .': (from a relief at Persepolis). See also p. 111.

The Great Invasion

5

The Ionians inhabited the Aegean coast of Asia Minor and thus occupied the western boundary of the Persian Empire. But they were Greeks, and their resentment of Persian rule finally erupted into the so-called Ionian Revolt (500–494 B.C.). The leader of the revolt was Aristagoras. He wanted the Greeks to intervene on the side of their Ionian kinsmen, and so he went to Sparta and Athens. It was the intervention of the Athenians which ultimately brought upon the Greeks the fury of the King of Persia, Darius.

How it All Began

So Aristagoras, ruler of Miletus on the Ionian coast, came to Sparta, where Cleomenes was king. Now the Spartans say that at the royal audience Aristagoras produced a map of the world, which showed all its lands, seas, and rivers engraved on bronze. 'Don't be surprised, King Cleomenes,' he said, 'that I am so eager to visit you. Circumstances compel me, because our slavery reflects almost as badly on you Spartans, as acknowledged leaders of Greece, as it does on ourselves. I beg you then in the name of the gods we both worship to help us liberate Ionia, since we are all your kinsfolk.'

He then went on to explain how easy it would all be, since the Barbarians—as he called the Persians—were cowards at heart, while the Spartans were the world's most renowned warriors. 'Those Persians fight with bows and arrows', he said, 'and tiny spears. They also wear trousers and pointed hats, which shows how useless they must be. But their country is richer than all the rest of the world put together in gold, silver, bronze, embroidered materials, animals, and slaves: and it is all yours for the taking. Look at this map and I'll show you where they all live.' And he began to describe them all: the Lydians with their silver-mines, the Phrygians and their rich agricultural land, Cappadocians, Cilicians, Armenians (famous for cattle), Matienians, Cissians, the river Choaspes with Susa standing on it, and Susa itself, the capital city where the Great King's treasure-chambers were. What a prize all that would be compared with the poor little parcels of land for which the Spartans were usually fighting their neighbours!

Cleomenes' reply was short and to the point: 'I'll give you an answer in two days' time', he said. So they met again on the appointed day and Cleomenes asked Aristagoras how far it was from the Ionian coast to Susa. Up to this point Aristagoras had kept his wits about him and had been quite clever about deceiving Cleomenes, but now he told the truth—a great mistake, if he ever wanted to persuade the Spartans to cross to Asia. 'Three months' march', he said, and was just about to go on and describe the route when Cleomenes cut him short. 'Be out of Sparta by sunset', he said. 'How ridiculous! Whoever heard of the Spartans marching such a long way from the coast?' And he strode out of the palace.

Aristagoras followed him and tried everything—prayers, supplications, entreaties. When they had all failed, he tried to persuade Cleomenes to send his nine-year-old daughter, Gorgo, out of earshot; but he was told to say what he liked in front of her. So he then offered Cleomenes 10 talents (i.e. 6000 drachmas or a day's pay for 12,000 Athenians) as a bribe to do what he asked. When this failed he raised his offer to 20 talents, and then on up to 50 talents; at which point Gorgo suddenly said in a loud voice: 'Be careful, father; he will corrupt you. Don't listen!'

Cleomenes took her advice and left the room. As for Aristagoras, he left Sparta for good and went off to Athens to try his luck there, since this was the second most powerful state in Greece. As it happened, the Athenians had just been in conflict with Artaphernes, the Persian satrap in Ionia. He wanted them to reinstate their banished tyrant Hippias, who had made friends with the Persians after his expulsion and was trying to use his influence with them to get himself restored. So far the Athenians had refused.

Aristagoras told them in their assembly the same old story as he had told the Spartans about the fabulous wealth of Asia and how useless the Persians were at fighting, because they did not use shields or proper spears and so on. He also gave them a long rigmarole about how Miletus had been founded by the Athenians, so that it was their duty to help their weaker kinsfolk. Indeed, by now he was so desperate for their help that he would have promised them anything under the sun; and finally he won them over. So it looks to me as if it is much easier to fool a whole people some of the time than a single person any of the time. For in fact 30,000 Athenians proved more gullible than one Spartan. They voted to send 20 warships to help the Ionians, together with their best general, Melanthius; and that decision was the start of all the trouble between the Greeks and the Persians.

When the Athenian fleet, accompanied by five allied ships from Eretria, reached Miletus, Aristagoras launched his expedition against Sardis, which since the defeat of Croesus had been the western capital of the Persian empire. He took care not to go himself, of course, but sent some other Milesian generals including his brother Charopinus. They marched via Ephesus, along the river Cayster, and across Mount Tmolus, and finally managed to take Sardis without opposition, apart from the main citadel which was defended by Artaphernes in person with a considerable force. But they got no plunder out of it all, because one of the soldiers set light to a building and the whole city went up in smoke, since the houses were all either made of reeds or at least thatched with them and so rapidly caught fire from each other.

When the news reached the Persian king, Darius, he seems to have ignored the Ionians' part in these happenings completely, presumably because he knew that they would soon pay the penalty for their revolt anyway. But he did inquire who these Athenians were. When he was told, he sent for his bow, seized hold of it, fitted an arrow to the string, pointed it up to heaven, and fired, calling to the king of the gods to grant him vengeance on the Athenians. Then he ordered one of his servants to say to him three times at every meal: 'Your Majesty, remember the Athenians.'

Marathon

The Ionian revolt was eventually suppressed in 494 B.C. By 490 Darius' preparations were complete and the Persian fleet carrying the invasion forces sailed off to exact vengeance from the enemies of Persia. It sailed via the Greek islands known as the Cyclades and made its final landfall at Marathon on the north coast of Attica. The Athenians, accompanied by their faithful allies from the town of Plataea, but not by the Spartans (who were delayed by a religious festival), watched the landing from the hills overlooking the Bay of Marathon.

Opinion in the Athenian high command was sharply divided. Some of the generals felt that their army was far too small to fight the Persians and they urged caution; others, like Miltiades, were for fighting. And indeed it looked as if the faint hearts would have their way, because the discussions had reached total deadlock. But there was still a chance. One person, other than the generals, was entitled to a vote in the War Council, and that was the Polemarch, or War Lord, an official chosen by lot but none the less traditionally given the same status as the ten elected generals. On this occasion the post was held by Callimachus of Aphidnae; so Miltiades went along to him and explained that he now had the power to make or break Athens. 'The choice is yours', he said. 'Do you want to go down in history as our greatest national hero, or as the man who betrayed us? This is the most deadly crisis Athens has ever had to face, and we know what to expect if we surrender: the Persians will hand us straight back to Hippias the tyrant—after which life will not be worth living at all. But if we beat them, we have the chance to become the greatest city in all Greece. And if you don't believe me when I tell you that you hold the key to Athens' whole future in your hands, I'll prove it to you; that is what I'm here for. The ten generals can't agree; five want to fight; five don't. And if we don't fight now, we'll have bitter disagreement in the city, our determination will disappear, and the traitors will have it all their own way. But if we attack now, before we go to pieces, with reasonable luck we can win the battle. It's all up to you—and only you. Support me, and you will keep Athens free and help to make her great. Support the others, who are all cowards, and we are ruined.'

Callimachus was convinced. He gave the casting vote, and the decision to fight was made. Each general was entitled to be supreme commander for one day, and each of those who had voted for fighting gave up his turn to Miltiades. He accepted this arrangement, but did not join battle until it was his own day to be in charge.

That day came. The Athenians lined up for battle. By convention, in those days, the Polemarch always commanded the right wing, so Callimachus took control there. He and his own troops led the way into the battle line, followed by the rest, so as to make one unbroken line. The Plataeans came last because they were

The plain of Marathon

to hold the left flank. In order to match the length of the Persian line the Athenians had made their own centre exceptionally thin and had concentrated the bulk of their forces on the wings. All was now ready; the omens looked good; the charge was sounded and they started off at a run towards the enemy, drawn up a full mile or more away.

The Persians watched them coming on fast and got ready for them. Obviously, they thought, these Athenians were suffering from suicidal mania to come rushing into the attack like that without cavalry and archers and with such a tiny army. But the Persians were quickly disillusioned. The Athenians struck, at the same instant, all along the line on a broad front and fought famously. They were the first Greeks, as far as I know, to charge an enemy like that and the first not to be terrified by the mere sight of Persian uniform. And on that day they proved, once and for all, that the Persian army could be beaten in battle.

A son goes to war: from the inside of a cup by the Brygos painter (about 450 B.C.). A popular subject, this picture reflects something of the humanity and intimacy which Persian art seems to lack.

For hours the fighting continued. In the centre, where the Sacae held the line together with the Persian crack troops, the enemy broke through, defeated the Greeks, and drove them back towards the hills. But on the wings the Athenians and the Plataeans were winning; and instead of pursuing the Barbarians as they ran for safety, they let them go, united their own two wings, and fell upon the successful Persian centre from behind and utterly destroyed them. The Persians ran for their lives, pursued by the Athenians, who cut them to pieces as they fled. They chased them all the way back to the water's edge, and then began to grab hold of the Persian ships, yelling for firebrands.

That was the great moment of climax which saw the death of the Polemarch, Callimachus; and a hero's death it was, too. Another general, Stesilaus, died beside him, while Euphorion's son, Cynegirus, had his hand chopped off by an axe while he was trying to seize hold of the stern of a ship. He too fell, along with many other well-known Athenians. All the same, they captured seven ships in this way, though the enemy managed to get the rest afloat and sailed off round the promontory of Sunium to the south, hoping to reach Athens before the Greek army returned. Athenian gossip says that the Alcmaeonids (see p. 90 ff.) were responsible for this idea: they were supposed to have flashed a signal with a shield in the sunlight to the enemy fleet while it was standing out to sea.

So while the Persians were sailing round Sunium, the Athenians were racing back to the city as fast as they could. They arrived there before the enemy and took up a defensive position in the grounds of the local temple of Heracles. The Persian fleet lay off Phalerum, the Athenian naval base, for a while and then sailed back to Asia, utterly demoralized by their defeat and the loss of their ships. They left behind 6,400 dead, compared with Athenian losses of 192.

Soon after this a Spartan task-force of 2000 men arrived, having travelled up from Sparta in such a hurry that it had taken them less than three days to reach Attica. But they were too late for the battle, of course. However, they were eager to see some Persians, even if they were only dead ones, so they all went to Marathon to have a look. After that, they congratulated the Athenians on their splendid victory—and went home again.

The distance from Marathon to Athens was approximately 42 kilometres and the distance of the modern race (26 miles 385 yards) was supposed to represent this, though in fact it was the distance from Windsor Park to the royal box in the White City Stadium where the 1908 games were held.

The race was instituted at the first modern Olympics, held in Athens in 1896, in honour of Pheidippides, the Greek soldier who is supposed to have run the 150 miles (240 km) from Athens to Sparta in 48 hours to fetch help, when the news came through of the Persian landings. Having raced back to fight at the battle of Marathon, he then ran the 42 kilometres to Athens to report victory, and on reaching the city fell dead, gasping out the news.

The Second Invasion: Persian Preparations

Darius died in 486 B.C., and so his plans for avenging the defeat at Marathon were thwarted. However, his young son and successor, King Xerxes, was just as eager to make the attempt. Once his intentions were known, the matter was hotly debated by his advisers in the Council. Mardonius, Darius' nephew, was strongly in favour. He was one of Persia's outstanding generals, and had helped to suppress the revolt of the Ionians. Later he was to be in charge of the elaborate combined operations involved in the invasion. Despite the opposition of Artabanus, Xerxes' uncle, they decided in favour and then left in order to scour the empire for troops and make preparations. It took four years, and in the fifth, 480 B.C., the army set out.

The Persian organization had been highly efficient. Food dumps had been prepared along the route; Greece had been infiltrated by spies; states had been bribed or terrorized into promising their support. Previous expeditions in the area had met with difficulties: one had nearly come to grief at the Hellespont, another had been wrecked off Mount Athos, where the prevailing wind from the north-east, which can get up very suddenly in the Aegean, had caught the fleet on a lee shore. So this time they were not going to allow such mistakes to happen; they decided to build a bridge across the Hellespont and cut a canal, about 2,300 metres long, through the isthmus behind Mount Athos.

Work had been going on here (at Athos) for the last three years under Bubares, son of Megabazus, and Artachaees, son of Artaeus. Men from every nation dug the canal, working on a shift system, driven by the lashes of their officers' whips and assisted by the local population who had been press-ganged into service. The Persians themselves surveyed and marked out the line of the canal from Sane at the northern end of the low isthmus that links Athos to the mainland and then shared out the digging among the various nations working on the project. They set up a central market in a meadow nearby and brought in massive supplies of ready-milled corn from Asia. I must confess that I cannot help thinking that Xerxes was suffering from some sort of megalomania in all this and wanted to show off his power, as well as leaving behind some sort of memorial of himself. He could so easily have dragged his ships across the isthmus on rollers, but he seems to have preferred to dig this huge channel, wide enough for two warships to row abreast.

However, work got under way and steadily the canal grew deeper, until those at the bottom were doing the digging and then passing the soil up to others standing above them on ladders; these passed it on again up the ladders until it reached the men standing at the top, who took it away and dumped it. Everyone except the Phoenicians had a lot of trouble with the sides of the canal, which kept crumbling and falling in because they had made the bottom and the top the same width. But the Phoenicians, who had shown themselves rather intelligent in one way or another, made the top of their section twice as wide as required, and then dug down at an angle till at the bottom their trench was the same width as everyone else's.

Meanwhile work was also going on at Abydus, a town situated on the Asian shore of the narrowest part of the Hellespont. From here to a headland on the other side Xerxes' engineers had built two pontoon bridges, one held together by cables of flax, the other by cables of papyrus, and each of them nearly a mile long. But when the work was already complete, a violent storm blew up which smashed the bridges and carried off the remains. Xerxes was furious when he heard the news, and he ordered the Hellespont to receive 300 lashes and to have a pair of fetters thrown into it. He is also said to have sent his torturers to brand it with red-hot irons and to have ordered the men with whips to make the following typically arrogant proclamation: 'You bitter waters, your Lord and Master punishes you thus because you have done him wrong, though he never wronged you. Nevertheless, Xerxes, High King of Persia, intends to cross your stream, whether you wish it or not. How right men are to refuse to sacrifice to a muddy and briny river like you.' After that, he ordered the engineers' heads to be chopped off (which was done—appalling as it may seem), and a second team settled down to build another pair of bridges. And this is how it was done.

They formed two parallel lines of warships lying side by side, with the sterns of each of the lines of ships facing each other. The ships were then lashed together and anchored fore and aft with extra-long anchors. Altogether there were 360 ships, triremes and penteconters, on the Black Sea side facing northeast into the current, and 314 on the Aegean side facing down the current and into the south-westerly gales, which are also common in those parts. This made sure that all the moorings

Phoenician warship: from a stele (engraved pillar) rather earlier than Salamis, commemorating Sennacherib's expedition to Phoenicia.

and cables remained taut wherever the wind came from. The builders also left a narrow gap in the lines of ships to allow small boats in and out of the Black Sea.

After that they stretched the main cables from shore to shore and pulled them tight with winches, this time using both kinds of cable at once, two of flax and four of papyrus for each line of ships. The thickness and efficiency of each type was about the same, but the flax ones were heavier since they weighed roughly one talent per cubit, that is about one hundredweight per metre. Once the bridges were complete, they sawed up tree-trunks to make planks equal to the length of the pontoons, laid them side by side on top of the now taut cables, and secured them there. On top of these they put a smooth layer of brushwood and covered

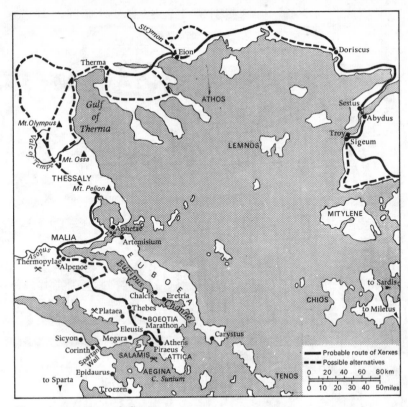

Xerxes' route through Greece

the whole with soil, which they hammered down hard before erecting a fence on both sides, so that the animals should not take fright when they saw the sea.

So now the bridges were ready. When news came that the Athos canal was also complete, the main army, which had spent the winter at Sardis, moved off in the early spring. As they were getting under way the sun vanished out of a cloudless sky and it turned as black as night. Alarmed at this, Xerxes asked his religious advisers what it all meant; but they assured him that it was heaven foretelling the eclipse of Greece, since the sun symbolized Greece and the moon Persia. Thus reassured, Xerxes ordered the expedition to start.

The 'Immortals' attending Xerxes at an audience—from the Hall of a Hundred Columns at Persepolis. Despite Herodotus' disparaging remarks, they were a fine and disciplined body of soldiers, as the night march over the mountains at Thermopylae proved.

The Persian Army

The statistics at the end of this next section are supported, in the text of Herodotus, by a wealth of detail. This has been omitted here, and only the total figures which he offers for each category are given. The figures are obviously much exaggerated; indeed, one modern scholar has calculated that if Herodotus' figures were right, the last units of Xerxes' army would still not have left Sardis by the time the first ones arrived at Thermopylae, where the first land battle took place. Another tells us that the experience of modern commanders suggests that the army could not have been as much as one-tenth of the size given in Herodotus. Nevertheless, it must have been a very large force indeed, and we need not be too severe on Herodotus for his inaccuracy, since his sources were certainly inaccurate too, for various reasons. First, it is natural to exaggerate one's successes and, because the Greeks were still a people whose only historical records before Herodotus were the memories of one generation handed down to the next—no doubt with improvements on the way—the size of the Persian army was bound to become steadily exaggerated over the years. Secondly, people in those days were never very accurate about large numbers; they did not regard it as important to be precise in such matters. An army was large, very large, or enormous: if it was enormous, then you produced numbers that would seem appropriate. Thirdly a people brought up on Homer's epics would feel it right to give the armies in an epic struggle epic proportions. And certainly it would suit Herodotus' chief purpose to believe them.

This was the biggest army the world has ever seen, far bigger than the one Darius led against the Scythians, bigger than the legendary army which Menelaus and Agamemnon took to Troy, bigger in fact than all the armies of legend and history put together. Every nation in Asia sent a contingent; they drank every river dry, except the really large ones. Some nations provided ships, others infantry, some cavalry, others transport ships and crews, some warships as pontoons for the bridges, others supplies and barges to carry them in. All these forces converged on Sardis and then marched to Abydus.

At this point an old man, who had served Xerxes well, asked, as a favour, that his eldest son should be allowed to stay at home and look after him, since all five of his sons were on the expedition. 'How dare you mention your son', exclaimed Xerxes, 'when I am marching against Greece with all my children, brothers, relatives, and friends? You are my slave; it is your duty to follow me with your whole household, even your wife, if necessary.' And he gave his men orders to find the man's son, slice him in two, and set up the two halves of his body on either side of the road, so that the army could march between them. And they did.

First came the baggage-carriers and the animals, and then the common soldiers from every nation under the sun, all mixed up together. After half the army had gone by, there was a gap, so that such people should have no contact whatsoever with the king's personal retinue. Then came 1,000 horsemen, the flower of the Persian cavalry, then 1,000 spearmen, the cream of the infantry, marching with spears reversed; then ten richly orna-mented horses from the Sacred Stables, then the holy chariot of the Supreme God drawn by eight white stallions with the charioteer marching on foot beside them holding the reins, since no mortal man may mount that chariot. Behind all this came Xerxes in a chariot drawn by horses from the great plain of Nisaea, with his driver, Patiramphes, son of Otanes, a Persian aristocrat.

Behind him marched 1,000 spearmen, the best and noblest in the land, with spears held high; then another 1,000, the pick of the Persian cavalry; then 10,000 infantry, the best of all that re-mained. Of these 1,000 had golden pomegranates on their spear butts, and 500 marched in front of and 500 behind the remaining 9,000, who had silver pomegranates. Then came 10,000 Persian cavalry and after them another interval of 400 metres. Then came the second half of the mass of common soldiers, again all mingled together.

They marched to Abydus, via Troy, where Xerxes sacrificed 1,000 oxen to the goddess Athene of Troy, and on arrival he decided he would like to inspect the whole army. A throne of white marble had already been set up for him on a hill, according to instructions, and there he sat and gazed towards the shore, where he could see at a glance the whole of his army and navy assembled. And when he saw the Hellespont completely covered with ships, and all the beaches and the plain of Abydus filled with men, Xerxes gave a smile of satisfaction—and burst into tears. When Artabanus asked him what was the matter, he replied, 'I was just thinking about the shortness of human life. Is it not tragic? All these men; and in a hundred years from now they will all be dead.' Then they prepared for the crossing of the Hellespont.

The next day, having waited for sunrise, they burned all sorts of incense on the bridge and spread myrtle boughs along the track. Then, as the sun came up, Xerxes poured wine from a sacred cup of gold as an offering into the sea, and prayed to the Sun not to allow any misfortune to stop him from conquering Europe and from marching to its furthest boundaries. Then he cast the cup, a golden mixing bowl, and a sword into the Hellespont, and the march began. The cavalry and the infantry went over by the upper bridge, the animals and the camp-followers by the lower. The 10,000 'Immortals' of the royal bodyguard, the crack regiment of Persia, led the way, with garlands on their heads, and after them came the general mass of troops. That took one day. On the next came the cavalry and the spearmen, garlanded like the 'Immortals'; after that the sacred horses, the Sacred Chariot, Xerxes, his spearmen, and his 1,000 horsemen; then the rest of the army. Meanwhile the ships moved across to the opposite shore simultaneously. For seven days and seven nights the crossing went on without ceasing, and then they all moved on to Doriscus, where Xerxes counted his troops. How many troops each nation provided I cannot say with any accuracy, since there are no satisfactory statistics available. But the infantry numbered in all 1,700,000. The method used to count them was to pack 10,000 together as tightly as possible into a single spot and then draw a circle round them. They were then dismissed and a fence was built, waist high, along the line of the circle. Then the rest of the army was marched into and out of the enclosed area until they had all been counted. And the number was, as I say, 1,700,000.

However, by the time the army had reached Thermopylae, its ranks had been swollen by allied contingents. So my final calculation is as follows:

Ships and Crews:	Warships	1,207	
	Men and marines per ship	230	
	Total number of men		277,610

	Other vessels	3,000
	Men per vessel (approx.)	80
	Total number of men	240,000
Infantry		1,700,000 (see previous page)
Cavalry		80,000
Plus:	Arabian camel drivers and Libyan charioteers	20,000
	Allied troops recruited *en route*	324,000
Grand Total of Fighting Men		2,641,610

But I reckon that camp followers of all kinds from officers'
servants to crews for the provision boats just about equalled the
number of front-line fighting troops.
So if we double the numbers of fighting men that Xerxes, son of
Darius, brought to Greece as far as the pass of Thermopylae we
find that the sum total is:

$$5,283,220$$

Artemisium and Thermopylae

The decision to hold Thermopylae (a narrow pass in northern
Greece, only 15 metres wide at one point) was one that the
Athenian leader, Themistocles, had been working hard to
bring about. Athens's chief allies, the Spartans, believed that
it would be better to build a wall across the Isthmus of Corinth
and fight there. But, as the Athenian admiral Themistocles
pointed out, that would not be much use if the Persians could
use their navy to sail round and deposit troops behind them.
Fighting at Thermopylae, however, would allow the Greeks to
prevent such tactics because the navy and army could make a
stand together, the army at Thermopylae and the navy in the
narrows between the island of Euboea and the mainland. They
could not then be outflanked, unless the Persians risked a long
row down the exposed outer coast of Euboea. There were other

advantages too. The Persian fleet would have two days of hard rowing along a treacherous coast from their previous anchorage in the Gulf of Therma. They would also have to spend one night at anchor on the open sea to get there. As the season of settled weather in the Aegean was nearly over, this was a risky thing to do—as events were to prove. In the end Themistocles had his way; the fleet moved up to Artemisium at the northern tip of Euboea and an advance party of 7,000 Spartans, under King Leonidas, marched north to Thermopylae in time to repair and fortify an ancient wall which was part of the defences that controlled the pass.

This decision was probably vital for the ultimate defeat of the Persian army, even though both these battles were lost. The Greeks had managed to unite for action; they had held up the Persian advance and inflicted heavy losses on them; they had certainly given the enemy tough and unexpected resistance. Herodotus thought it was even more important than that, and it is worth quoting him at some length.

At this point I feel compelled to state an opinion which will be widely disapproved of by many people; but I must give it because I think it is true. If the Athenians had lost their nerve at the approach of danger and had either abandoned Greece or merely stayed where they were and surrendered to Xerxes, no one would have tried to resist him on the sea at all. And without naval resistance it would have been inevitable that in the end the Spartans would have been left to fight on their own by their allies, who would have had no choice but to betray them, however many defensive walls they built across the Isthmus, because the Persians would have been able to defeat those allies one at a time.

Of course the Spartans would have died heroically; or possibly, once they saw the rest of Greece was giving in, they would have come to terms with Xerxes. But whatever they did, Greece would have become Persian territory. For as long as the king had command of the sea, there was no possible point that I can see in building walls across the Isthmus.

This leads to the inevitable conclusion that Athens saved Greece and that the result depended entirely on what course of action the Athenians chose to take. And having chosen to defend the freedom of the Greeks, it was the Athenians who roused the rest of them to fight and not to surrender. In fact they were second only to the gods in driving out the King of Persia.

In the meantime Xerxes was marching south from Therma and eleven days later his fleet followed, timing its departure to allow it to rendezvous with the army at Thermopylae. They moored for the night somewhere off Mount Pelion and in the early morning were caught by a violent storm which raged for three days and, according to Herodotus, 'wrecked at least 400 ships'. However, enough remained of Xerxes' fleet not to deter him in any way. His army was now arriving at Thermopylae, his fleet was limping into shelter past the temple of Artemis (on the northern tip of Euboea), which gave its name to the battle; the scene was set for the two battles—the naval battle of Artemisium and the heroic struggle for the narrow pass of Thermopylae.

Artemisium

These were the states who contributed to the Greek fleet which fought at Artemisium: Athens—127 ships (including crews from their allied city of Plataea, who had volunteered for service out of sheer courage and patriotism, even though they had never sailed a ship before), Corinth—40 ships, Megara—20, Chalcis—20 crews only, the ships being supplied by Athens, Aegina—18, Sicyon—12, Sparta—10, Epidaurus—8, Eretria—7, Troezen—5, Styra—2, Ceos—2 ships and 2 galleys, Opuntian Locris—7 galleys. So, apart from the galleys, the grand total of ships which fought at Artemisium was 271.

The supreme commander was a Spartan, Eurybiades, because the allies had refused to serve under an Athenian admiral and insisted on a Spartan, threatening to break up the proposed expedition altogether if they did not get their way. The Athenians had, therefore, agreed to the general wish, since they reckoned that the survival of Greece was more important than their own prestige and that if there was a quarrel about who was to be admiral, Greece would be destroyed. They were quite right, of course: for although war is a much more unpleasant thing than peace, internal quarrelling within a nation is far worse than a war waged by a united country.

When the fleet reached Artemisium, they saw large numbers of Persian ships drawn up at Aphetae across the bay and the whole place swarming with Persian troops. This took them rather by surprise, since it was obvious that the Persians had survived the storm off Mt. Pelion a good deal better than the Greeks had expected. They were, indeed, sufficiently shaken to consider an immediate withdrawal to the south again. But when the local people living on Euboea discovered their intentions, they begged Eurybiades to stay for a while, long enough at least for them to evacuate their children and slaves to a place of safety. When he refused they turned to Themistocles, the Athenian admiral, and persuaded him to get the fleet to stay and fight at Artemisium in return for a bribe of 30 talents. He promptly passed on 5 talents to Eurybiades, pretending that it was a personal gift from himself. That was enough to change the Spartan admiral's mind, and the only other opposition came from the Corinthian admiral, Adeimantus. So Themistocles assured Adeimantus that he himself would pay him more for staying loyal to his friends than Xerxes would ever give him for deserting them—and he sent direct to his ship three talents of silver. This disposed of the opposition, satisfied the Euboeans, and made a large profit for Themistocles too. No one knew about it, of course, since the two bribed admirals imagined that the money had come from Athens specially for the purpose of 'persuading' them. But the result was that the fleet did stay and fight at Artemisium, which was what Themistocles had wanted in the first place.

The rest of the Persians, arriving during the early afternoon, saw with their own eyes that the rumours they had heard were true and that it really was a tiny Greek fleet that had assembled at Artemisium. This made them all the more eager to attack at once and capture them quickly if they could. But they decided not to make an immediate assault, since it was already late afternoon and they did not want the Greeks to run away when they saw them coming and so escape under cover of the approaching night. Certainly escape was likely, and since the Persian policy was to 'take no prisoners', escape had to be prevented. So what they did was to detach a squadron and order it to sail all round the outside of Euboea and up into the Euripus from the south (the Euripus being the narrow channel between Euboea and the mainland). In this way they would be able to cut off the Greeks' retreat from behind while their main force attacked from in front. And so, in accordance with this plan, they sent off a detachment of 200 ships and agreed not to make any attack until they had received a pre-arranged signal to say that the Euripus squadron was in position. Meanwhile they filled in time by holding a review of the fleet.

However, there was a man in the Persian fleet called Scyllias, the best swimmer and diver in Greece. He had long wanted to desert his Persian masters but had so far not had a chance. How he managed to reach the Greek camp on this occasion I cannot say for certain, though I have my doubts about the popular account, which claims that he dived into the sea at Aphetae and did not surface again until he reached Artemisium, having travelled under water for a distance of 10 miles. There are a number of equally far-fetched stories told about him, and others as well that are probably true. My own opinion is that this time he arrived by boat. But the important thing is that on arrival he immediately gave the naval commanders full details of the shipwreck off Mt. Pelion and the movements of the Euripus squadron which was sailing round Euboea at that moment.

This information led to intense discussions among the Greeks. They finally decided to stay at their moorings for the rest of the day and then set out at about midnight in order to surprise the Euripus squadron as it came up behind them. But it never arrived, and having waited till the late afternoon they finally sailed back and attacked the main Persian fleet instead, so as to try and find out what they were like under battle conditions. When Xerxes and his admirals saw this tiny fleet sailing out to attack them, they decided the Greeks must be quite mad and hurriedly got under way themselves, thinking they would easily capture them all—a reasonable assumption under the circumstances, since the Greek numbers were small and their own ships more numerous and faster. So they came out to battle in a rather contemptuous frame of mind, expecting to encircle their opponents and trap them without much trouble. The Greeks were a well-disciplined force: at a given signal they formed a tight circle of ships; at a second signal they launched a frontal attack, despite the cramped conditions which left them little room for manoeuvre. The battle itself proved indecisive and ended at nightfall with the Greeks pulling back to Artemisium and some very surprised Persians to Aphetae. The only Greek to desert from the Persian side on this occasion was Antidorus, from the island of Lemnos, and for this the Athenians rewarded him with a small property on the island of Salamis.

That night there was an unusually severe midsummer storm

with heavy rain, and a savage thunderstorm over Mt. Pelion. Corpses and bits of wreckage came floating into Aphetae bay all night, getting caught up and entangled with the oars of the Persian ships lying there and frightening the life out of the Persian sailors, who after all their other misfortunes now expected to die at any minute. For they had barely recovered from the first storm off Mt. Pelion which had wrecked so many of their ships, they had been forced to fight a severe sea-battle that day, and now they were in the middle of a wild storm and a cloudburst; the local streams were all suddenly bursting their banks and pouring down into the sea, and a terrible thunderstorm was rolling round them.

But for their Euripus squadron on its way round Euboea that same night was a far more disastrous experience. The storm caught these ships out on the open sea and the crews met a most unpleasant death. It struck while they were off the southern tip of Euboea, a place called the Hollows; it was a strange coast to them and the gale drove them straight onto the rocks. In fact in this war the gods seemed to have been doing all they could to even up the odds which were at first so heavily in favour of the Persians with their vastly superior numbers.

As for the Persian fleet at Aphetae, they were delighted to see the light of day once more, and stayed exactly where they were all day, quite happy to relax after the battering they had suffered. The Greeks, however, had received reinforcements of 53 ships from Athens and these, together with the news of the total destruction of the Euripus squadron off Euboea, brought a surge of optimism to their sailors. Once again, as on the previous day, they waited until mid-afternoon and then fell upon some Cilician ships, which they destroyed before withdrawing once more to Artemisium at nightfall.

The Persian admirals by this time were furious that a tiny fleet should have done them so much damage; they were also rather anxious about Xerxes' reactions to these continual set-backs. So on the third day they did not give the Greeks a chance to attack but made their own preparations and then launched an attack at midday. This assault coincided with the third day of the land forces' attack on Thermopylae, and of course, the objectives of the two sides in each battle were identical: at Artemisium and Thermopylae (where King Leonidas and his men were) the Greeks were fighting to prevent the Persians breaking through into Greece proper by defending a narrow passage—the straits at Artemisium and the pass of Thermopylae. The Persians, likewise, were trying in each case to destroy the Greeks holding the two passages and so force their way through. Xerxes' fleet took more trouble to get properly organized this time and then sailed towards the Greeks who were waiting for them off Artemisium. They ordered their wings to move up ahead of the rest in crescent formation so as to overlap the enemy flanks. But the moment they saw this manoeuvre the Greeks promptly launched another frontal attack, and so the battle began. It was a more even struggle than the numbers would have suggested, since the sheer size of Xerxes' fleet meant that it did almost as much damage to itself as the Greeks did because of the confusion caused by crowds of ships bumping into each other all the time. But they did fight well all the same, and in their determination not to be driven back by smaller numbers they refused to give way at all. Nevertheless, though the Greeks lost a large number of men and ships, the Persians lost far more. In the end the honours of this battle were roughly even and both sides withdrew and returned to their moorings with considerable relief. The Greeks, however, did at least manage to recover their corpses and damaged ships once the battle was over, but they had suffered heavily, especially the Athenians who had lost half their fleet. So they decided to escape to the south while they still had a chance and reorganized their forces at Salamis, the island off the coast of Attica, ready for the most decisive battle of the war.

Thermopylae

The Persian army was now approaching and the Greeks at Thermopylae suddenly lost their nerve and started to think about retreating. Most of the Spartans and their allies thought they should withdraw back to the Peloponnese and hold the Isthmus. But Leonidas and a few others were furious at this suggestion and successfully persuaded the rest to send urgent messages to their allies demanding reinforcements, since their numbers were too small to hold out for long.

Meanwhile Xerxes sent a mounted scout forward to spy out the enemy's numbers and activities. The scout rode forward to-

A Greek hoplite with his long spear, heavy shield, and crested helmet defeats a trousered Persian; despite what Herodotus says on p. 95, it was not the trousers but the inadequate weapons and armour that made the Persians such poor soldiers at close quarters.

wards the Greek position and carefully inspected everything as far as he could, though the Greek encampment was only partially visible, the rest of it being obscured by the now reconstructed wall. He was rather surprised to see that the men on outpost duty in front of the wall—Spartans as it happened—were stripped for exercise or combing their hair; certainly none of them took the slightest notice of him. So he made an accurate assessment of their numbers, noted all the other details, and rode quietly away to tell Xerxes what he had seen. The king did not know what to make of it at all, so he questioned one of his Greek advisers, Demaratus, son of Ariston. 'Your Majesty,' he replied, 'I told you about these men when we set out; I predicted what would happen and you laughed at me. Now I promise you that I

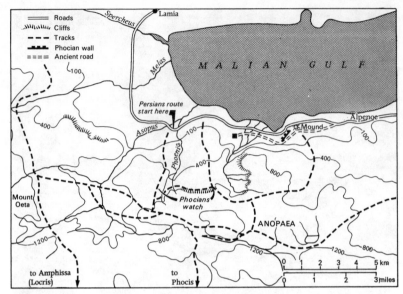

Thermopylae

am only trying to tell you the facts, so please listen. These Spartans have come here determined to fight you for the possession of this pass and they are preparing for battle in their traditional way. Whenever they are about to risk their lives, they take great pains to comb their hair beautifully. If only you can defeat them and the rest of their forces back in Sparta, no other nation on earth will lift a finger against you. They have the finest kingdom in Greece and the bravest warriors. Call me a liar if my forecast is wrong.'

But Xerxes did not believe him and waited for four days to see if the Greeks would run away. By the fifth day he was irritated by what seemed to him an example of utter stupidity on the part of the Greeks, so he sent the Medes and Cissians into the attack with orders to take them alive, because he wanted to have a look at these madmen. The Medes charged into the attack and were driven back with enormous losses; others took their place, but for all their efforts they could not dislodge the Spartans. As anyone could see, including the king, the Persian army had plenty of manpower but not much manhood. All day long the battle raged and the Medes were badly mauled. Finally Xerxes called in the 'Immortals', his crack regiment, and they advanced as though they at least were going to make short work of these Spartans. But they did no better than the Medes, and met exactly the same problems: a narrow pass, spears much too short, and inability to use their superior numbers.

But that does not mean that the Spartans did not put up a great fight; they did. After all, they were seasoned soldiers fighting raw recruits, and were able to use, as one of their tactics, the trick of turning their backs and pretending to run away, which sent the Barbarians clattering after them with whoops of joy. When they had drawn them forward to the planned position, the Spartans would turn round and cut them to pieces. Persian casualties were appalling; the Spartans' negligible. At last the Persians realized that they were getting nowhere and withdrew. As for Xerxes, in watching the course of the battle he is supposed to have leapt from his throne three times in an agony of terror for his troops.

The next day the Persians attacked again, hoping this time that the Greeks with their small numbers might have suffered too many casualties to be able to carry on. The result, however, was exactly the same as on the previous day. Xerxes was in difficulties—and he knew it. But at that moment a man from Malia asked to see the king. His name was Epialtes and, hoping to get a rich reward, he told the king about a track which ran through the mountains to Thermopylae round the back. He was the traitor who sold the Greeks for gold; and he died later, an exile, with a price upon his head.

Xerxes was delighted, and in great excitement selected Hydarnes and the 'Immortals' for the expedition. They left camp as dusk was falling and followed the track from where it begins at the river Asopus, which flows through a gorge under the mountain called, like the track itself, Anopaea. This track follows the spine of the mountain as far as the town of Alpenoe, stopping where the road is narrowest, at the so-called Black-Buttock Rock and Goblins' Chairs. This was the route followed that night by the Persians, and dawn found them on the main ridge of the mountain at the very point where a detachment of 1,000 Phocian volunteers had been left by Leonidas to guard the track, which also led to their own country. All the way up the Persians had been hidden by the oak-woods which covered the mountain, and the first the Phocians knew about them was when they reached the ridge. In the breathless hush of the early morning the rustle of leaves under foot naturally made a considerable noise; but while the startled Phocians were still scrambling into their equipment, the Persians were already upon them. They were somewhat surprised to find any opposition at all, let alone an armed force ready to resist. Indeed, Hydarnes even thought they might be Spartans, but he checked up with Epialtes and having been told the facts moved straight into the attack. As for the Phocians, once they came under heavy fire from the Persian archers, they fled to the top of the mountain, and, assuming that they themselves were the focal point of the attack, prepared to sell their lives dearly. But the Persians ignored them entirely after that and headed off down the track at full speed. The first hint of danger to reach the Greeks at Thermopylae came from their soothsayer, Megistias, who said that the signs foretold that death was coming in the morning. Then, during the night, deserters came in with the news of the Persians' flanking movement; finally, in the early dawn, the look-out men from the hill-tops came racing down with the news. An immediate council of war followed at which there was again a sharp division of opinion. Some said it was their duty to stay and fight; others disagreed. As a result the army divided: some left and went home; others prepared to stand and die with Leonidas.

As the sun came up Xerxes poured drink-offerings to it and waited, as Epialtes had suggested, till about 8 o'clock before moving forward. And as his troops advanced, the Greek forces round Leonidas, knowing that they were going out to die, made a much deeper sally than usual into a more open section of the pass. There they joined battle and before their assault the Barbarians fell in thousands. At the back the Persian officers had to use whips to drive the men forward. Many fell into the sea and were drowned; still more were trampled to death underfoot. No one could count how many died that day. The Greeks, who realized that the enemy was coming down from the hills behind them, fought with the mad recklessness of men who know that death is inevitable. By now most of their spears were broken, so they cut the Persians down with their swords.

Leonidas, the hero of the battle, fell at this point, with many a Spartan noble at his side, and a tremendous struggle developed over his corpse, until, finally, the Greeks routed their enemies for the fourth time and dragged his body clear. So it went on, until Epialtes approached with the 'Immortals'.

Once they knew these were approaching, the Greeks changed their tactics and withdrew to the narrowest part of the pass again. They left the wall and took up a position on a small hill to one side in close formation, at the entry to the pass where the stone lion still stands to this day in memory of Leonidas. And on this spot they fought to the bitter end: with swords, if they still had them, with hands and teeth if not, till the Barbarians, coming at them from all sides, finally overwhelmed them by sheer weight of numbers. They were buried where they fell and over the Spartans who died beside Leonidas this epitaph still stands:

> Go home and tell the Spartans, passer-by,
> We chose to follow orders, and to die.

Salamis

The actions at Artemisium and Thermopylae had slowed down the Persian advance, but that was all. Herodotus reckons that reinforcements easily made up for the losses they had suffered 'in the storm, at Thermopylae, and at Artemisium', and that additional troops continued to join them at every stage of their advance. Meanwhile they pressed on southwards into Attica, occupied Athens, which had been abandoned by its citizens without resistance, and seized, sacked, and burned the Acropolis, which was the only part of the city to be defended at all—and that was by a mere handful of resolute men who had refused to join the general evacuation.

After this Xerxes turned his attention to the Greek fleet which, also reinforced, was holding the strait between Salamis island and the mainland (see map p. 124). Herodotus' narrative is not always clear and if you want a detailed examination of what seems to have happened in the battle that followed—and indeed in the whole Persian campaign—you should read A. R. Burn's *Persia and the Greeks*. But you can see from the map that it would have been perfectly possible for Xerxes to ignore the Greek fleet entirely and sail straight for the Peloponnese so as to make a landing behind the defensive wall which the allies were by then frantically building across the Isthmus to keep him out. Indeed, this was the advice that, according to Herodotus, was actually given to Xerxes by Artemisia, his very distinguished female sea-captain. Her argument was that if he ignored the Greek fleet and landed on the Peloponnese they would rapidly disperse because of hunger (since there were very limited supplies on Salamis) and also through anxiety among the Peloponnesian members to get back and defend their homeland instead of Athens. She may well have been right. Certainly in Herodotus' narrative there is a report of another fierce debate in the Greek high command about whether they should or should not hold the Salamis narrows. As usual, he gives the credit for the vital decision to fight there to an Athenian, Themistocles. But, also as usual, Themistocles had to use deceit to get his own way. This time he sent a secret and apparently treacherous message to the Persians telling them to block the back exit from the Salamis channel, since the Greeks were just about to run away and would all escape. The Persians took his 'advice' and so the Greeks had to stay and fight where they were.

That is Herodotus' account of what happened. But in fact Xerxes very probably did not dare to attack the Peloponnese while such a large fleet was free to attack his line of communications. It was essential to have control of the sea for bringing up supplies, since the land route through Greece was over difficult terrain and through hostile territory. He, therefore, had to challenge the Greek fleet first—and the battle of Salamis, the most vital battle of the whole war, was the result of his decision to do so.

The Greek land forces were now at the Isthmus, slaving away to build their defensive wall and firmly believing that the whole outcome of the war would now depend on their efforts. They certainly did not expect the navy to make any further significant contribution. As for the men of the fleet, now at Salamis, they were alarmed to hear what their friends at the Isthmus were doing, not because they feared for their own lives but rather because it reminded them of the danger now threatening the Peloponnese. However, for a time they simply grumbled to each other about the unbelievable folly of their admiral, Eurybiades, in refusing to retreat; but in the end their anxieties turned into public criticism of his tactics.

As a result, needless to say, another meeting was held, which led to another long debate in the high command, with one group demanding that they should sail for the Peloponnese at once and make their final stand there rather than stay to defend a country that was already lost, while the Athenians, Aeginetans, and Megarians insisted that they should stay where they were. Themistocles, the Athenian, had a shrewd suspicion that they might be outvoted by the Peloponnesian group, so he slipped quietly out of the meeting and sent one of his own personal slaves, called Sicinnus, in a boat across to the Persian camp with a message and precise instructions about what he was to say. He was to tell them that he had been sent by the Athenian admiral, who was a secret supporter of theirs, and explain that the Greeks were now thoroughly frightened and were planning to escape, and that this gave the Persians a golden opportunity which they must not miss. The Greek fleet was torn by disagreements and would offer no resistance—indeed, they would soon be tearing each other to pieces.

The Persians, of course, believed the whole story, and Sicinnus slipped away, his job done. Later Themistocles rewarded him for this by making him a rich man and a citizen of Thespia, at a time when the Thespians were looking for men to swell their numbers and were enrolling new citizens. As for the Persians, the first thing they did was to put a strong force ashore on the small but strategically placed island of Psyttaleia. Then once it was pitch dark, they dispatched the west wing of their fleet in a pincer movement round Salamis to block the Greek escape route, while the squadrons positioned off Ceos and Cynosura moved forward and sealed off the whole strait in front as far as Munychia. Thus they hoped to prevent the Greeks escaping and, by forcing them to stay and fight in the narrows, avenge the losses of Artemisium.

Meanwhile that night among the Greek commanders at Salamis there was a fierce argument going on. They were not yet aware that they had been trapped by the Persians who, as far as they knew, were still occupying the same positions as during the day. However, while their discussions were still totally deadlocked, an Athenian called Aristeides arrived, having sailed across from the island of Aegina. He was an aristocrat who had been banished from Athens by the popular democratic party, which was led by Themistocles. But I believe from what I know of him that he was one of her best and most honourable citizens. For even though Themistocles was his most bitter political opponent, on this occasion Aristeides was willing to forget the past because of the enormous danger threatening them all. He knew that the Peloponnesians were eager to retreat to the Isthmus, and so he now went to the high command as they were sitting in council and asked Themistocles to come out and have a word with him. There he explained that all the Peloponnesian talk about retreat was futile, since he had seen with his own eyes that they were all now surrounded. Themistocles explained that this was just the news he wanted to hear but that if he reported it himself, the Peloponnesians would only think he was making it up. So he persuaded Aristeides to come in and make his report in person. This he did, explaining that he had just come across from Aegina, having had considerable difficulty in slipping through the blockading forces, since the whole fleet was now completely surrounded. He urged them all to get ready to fight at once, since escape was clearly impossible. But this led to another argument, since most of the commanders refused to believe him. However in the end a ship from Tenos, deserting from the Persians, arrived, and its captain confirmed Aristeides' report. So the Greeks got ready for action. At dawn Themistocles made a speech to encourage the assembled crews, then gave the order to embark; and the whole fleet got under way.

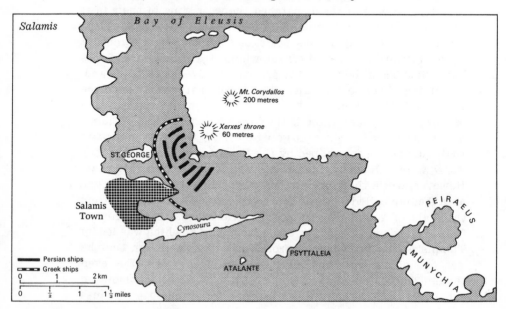

Now the Athenians say that right at the very start of the action, Adeimantus, the Corinthian admiral, lost his nerve and in sheer terror hoisted his sails and fled, followed by the rest of his fleet. Of course the Corinthians deny this! But certainly, when the fleet got under way and the Persian assault began, the Greeks' first reaction was to back water and make for the shore again. But Ameinias of Pallene, an Athenian, pressed forward, and rammed an enemy ship; this brought the Greek fleet out again to help and so the battle began in earnest.

Now although I cannot give accurate details of how the various Greek and Persian crews performed, I can give the following details about Artemisia's achievements, which greatly increased her reputation with Xerxes. During the battle, at a time when the Persian fleet had been reduced to complete disorder, Artemisia's ship was being pursued by an Athenian one and could not escape because one of her allies' ships was blocking the way. It was, as it happened, the flagship of Damasithymus of the Calyndians, and whether Artemisia had some private grudge against him or it was just blind chance I do not know, but she rammed and sank it without trace. The result was lucky for her in two ways: the pursuing Greek captain promptly decided that she was either a Greek ship or a deserter and turned his attention elsewhere, and so she escaped; and Xerxes, who happened to see the incident, was told by his staff that she was fighting heroically and had rammed an enemy ship. Luckily no one survived from the Calyndian ship to reveal the truth. Xerxes' reaction to all this was to complain bitterly that his men had all become women and his women men.

Amongst those killed in the battle were Xerxes' brother, the general Ariabignes, and a large number of other Persian, Median, and allied nobles—but very few Greeks, since, unlike the Persians, they all knew how to swim: so anyone not killed in the fighting swam to safety on Salamis. But large numbers of Persians drowned and when their leading ships turned to flee, those coming up behind in a desperate effort to get to the front and do some splendid service for their king became tangled up with the retreating ships and contributed further to the general slaughter and destruction. In the resulting chaos some of the Phoenicians whose ships had been destroyed accused the Ionians, quite falsely, of betraying them and ramming their ships. But while they were making this accusation in front of the king, an Ionian ship from Samothrace managed to sink an Athenian. And as she was going down, up came an Aeginetan ship and sank the Samothracian. Thereupon the Samothracian crew, being all skilled javelin-throwers, launched a volley of javelins from their sinking ship which cleared the Aeginetan's deck completely. They then leaped aboard and captured the ship. When Xerxes saw this remarkable performance, he turned on the Phoenicians and in his frantic search for scapegoats furiously ordered their heads to be chopped off for slandering men who were obviously far better than themselves.

So the battle ended and the Persians turned to flee. But as they made for Phalerum the Aeginetan fleet was waiting for them in the narrows. The result was devastating. In the general confusion the Athenians destroyed anyone that tried to resist or run away; and if they did manage to escape, the Aeginetans caught them as they emerged from the straits. So anyone who got away from the Athenians fell into the clutches of the Aeginetans. Such Persian ships as finally escaped limped back into Phalerum and joined forces with the land army once more.

Xerxes Goes Home

> Since the campaigning season was over Xerxes hurried home. But he left his general, Mardonius, with a large hand-picked army to renew the struggle in the following year.

Xerxes left Mardonius in Thessaly and marched at full speed for the Hellespont with the remainder of his army, which was not much. They lived as best they could off the country, eating grass and the leaves or bark from trees, taking whatever they could get. They were stricken by disease and dysentery, and when they reached the Hellespont they found the bridges wrecked by storms and had to cross by boat. When they got to Abydus, they found a better food-supply than they had had on the march, and many of them died from over-eating or the effects of the change of water.

But Xerxes himself only stayed with the army as far as Eion on the River Strymon. Here he took a Phoenician ship to sail direct to Asia. On the way a gale blew up and the sea rose alarmingly. The ship was overloaded and top-heavy, with crowds of Persians from Xerxes' retinue packing the decks. In his alarm Xerxes asked the captain what hope there was for any of them. 'None whatever, my Lord,' was the answer, 'unless we can get rid of all those passengers.' At this Xerxes turned to his followers and said, 'Gentlemen of Persia, now you all have a chance to prove your loyalty. It lies within your power to save the life of your king.'

At this the Persians each bowed low before him and leapt into the sea, and the boat, having thus jettisoned her cargo, reached Asia safely. As soon as he had landed Xerxes gave the captain a gold crown for saving the life of the King of Persia. Then he chopped off his head for losing the lives of so many of his nobles.

In the following year, 479, the two sides met for the last time—at Plataea, a small town on the borders of Attica. The Greeks won, thanks to superior Spartan discipline and armour. That ended the Persian threat, although next the Greeks took the initiative and, led by Athens, formed a league to ravage Persian territory and recoup their own losses. But the Spartans soon retired behind their borders and came out again only when the league, becoming virtually an Athenian empire, threatened their interests. The result was war once more, this time Athens against Sparta; later there was war with Thebes; later again with Macedonia. The Greeks never really recaptured that brief but glorious unity which helped defeat their common enemy, Persia.

Memorial to the Spartans at Thermopylae

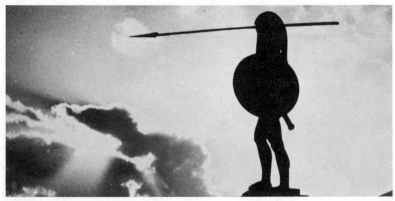

List of References

Many of the passages in this book have been edited and shortened. Nevertheless, the following list will be useful to those who want to know where to read them in the original.